RETURNING TO THE SOURCE

RETURNING TO THE SOURCE

Daoist Meditations for Rediscovering the Sacred in Everyday Life

SOLALA TOWLER

SHAMBHALA

Shambhala Publications, Inc.
2129 13th Street
Boulder, Colorado 80302
www.shambhala.com

Cover art: Q3kiaPictures/Shutterstock and Claire Chien/Shutterstock
Cover design: Daniel Urban-Brown
Interior design: Anna Becker

9 8 7 6 5 4 3 2 1

First Edition
Printed in the United States of America

Shambhala Publications makes every effort to print
on acid-free, recycled paper.
Shambhala Publications is distributed worldwide
by Penguin Random House, Inc., and its subsidiaries.

LIBRARY OF CONGRESS CATALOGING-IN-PUBLICATION DATA
Names: Towler, Solala author
Title: Returning to the source: Daoist meditations for rediscovering
the sacred in everyday life / Solala Towler.
Description: First edition. |Boulder, Colorado: Shambhala Publications, [2026] |
Identifiers: LCCN 2025036652 | ISBN 9781645475088 trade paperback
Subjects: LCSH: Meditation—Taoism
Classification: LCC BL1923 .T69 2026 | DDC 299.5/1444—dc23/eng/20251118
LC record available at https://lccn.loc.gov/2025036652

The authorized representative in the EU for product safety and compliance is
eucomply OÜ, Pärnu mnt 139b-14, 11317 Tallinn, Estonia,
hello@eucompliancepartner.com.

CONTENTS

INTRODUCTION

PEOPLE HAVE BEEN MEDITATING for thousands of years. Of course they probably have not always called it meditation. They may have used terms like *stillness,* or *going within,* or *being quiet so the animals will come to us.* Shamans used this stillness practice to break through the veil of life and death, allowing them to journey into other worlds, worlds that intersect ours and are filled with spirit beings. Of course they also used drumming and dancing, but it was the still place within them that allowed them to travel to the spirit lands to bring back guidance, information, and inspiration to share with their tribe, their family, and their beloved ones.

Yogis in India, monks in the West, Daoist (Taoist) hermits and wanderers, and Buddhists in Tibet, China, and Japan have all used meditation for eons to balance and strengthen their inner power and connect to what the Chinese call Dao or Source and what other peoples have called God, Allah, Brahma, or the Great Mystery.

Many people practice a form of meditation today that is not associated with any religion. This is all well and good. Anything that gets you to quiet your mind and take some slow, deep breaths cannot but help you.

The meditation practices I will be offering in this small book come from the great tradition of Daoism. But in truth, you do not have to convert to Daoism to benefit from them.

I do think that knowing a little about where they come from is good, hence the chapter "Embracing the One" that follows this introduction.

Much of what we think of today as traditional Chinese culture comes from Daoism. Landscape painting, calligraphy, feng shui, acupuncture, herbalism, *an mo* and *tuina* massage, *qigong* (chi gong), *taiji* (tai chi), food combining, tea ceremony, meditation, poetry, music, and more have all been heavily influenced or have come directly from Daoist philosophy and practice.

For many people, meditation has connotations of sitting stiffly for hour upon hour, striving vainly to stop all thoughts, while your legs either fall asleep or are wracked with pain. This is not the kind of meditation I will be sharing here. The beauty of Daoist meditation is that one can do it sitting, standing, moving, or even lying down. There does not have to be any pain involved, and if there is, you just need to adjust your posture, your position, or the type of meditation you are practicing.

No matter what shape you are in—physically, psychologically, emotionally, or even spiritually—there is a type of Daoist meditation that will work for you. I will be sharing many types with you. I suggest you try a few of them out before settling on one or two that are right for you at this time. At another time, you may want to change or adjust the meditation practice that is correct for you as you move along your own journey to healing.

Most important, it is best to not come to Daoist meditation with any preconceptions about what meditation can do for you or to you. As in all important things, keeping an open mind and open heart and having a willingness to explore new facets of your own consciousness are the two things that will help you so much on your journey toward wholeness, healing, and spiritual transformation.

All quotations from Laozi's (Lao Tzu's) *Daodejing* and from Master Zhuang's (Chuang Tzu's) *Zhuangzi* are from my previous books.

HOW TO USE THIS BOOK

This book is primarily a series of guided meditations. You can refer to the book as you practice or even record some meditations to follow along to your own voice. It is very important that you take your time with each step of any meditation, really feel that you are following along in a slow and deep way, and find your own rhythm and pace. One of the most important principles in Daoist practice is *manzou*, going slowly. There is no need to rush through any of the practices.

You may find that you are attracted to certain practices more than others. That is all well and good. You can certainly do a few or even one of the meditations over and over. As a matter of fact, they will be that much more powerful that way.

Many of these practices grew out of the weekly meditation classes that I have been leading for the last six years. In other words, I got to try them out in real time before I put them to paper. I am so happy now to be able to share them with a wider audience with the help of the good people at Shambhala Publications!

A word on the spelling of Chinese terms: I follow the modern transliteration system, pinyin, which is used in contemporary China and by most international scholars. In this system, the words are mostly spelled the way they are pronounced. In the old Wade–Giles system, the word *Dao* is spelled with a "T" (Tao) but pronounced as a "D," which is very confusing for Western readers. So now we spell it with a "D." Likewise, the name of the author of the *Daodejing* is spelled Laozi and pronounced as it is spelled, "Lao zeh." There are still a few problems with this modern system, as with the term *qigong,* which is pronounced "chee goong." So it is not perfect but still much better than the old system.

RETURNING TO THE SOURCE

1

Embracing the One

Who can remain still and quiet while the mud settles?
Who can remain calm and still until it is time to move?[1]

—*DAODEJING*

Let meditation assist your life;
do not use it to spin a cocoon around your life.[2]

—HUA-CHING NI

Soft like a cloud,
solid like a mountain,
I sit and await the unfolding.

—BAI YUN

WHEN PEOPLE HEAR THE TERM *MEDITATION*, they often think of an austere practice of sitting in an uncomfortable position for an interminable time, trying very hard not to think of anything as the mind races madly and the legs and back cramp up. Or they may think of sitting high in the mountains, leaving their earthly forms behind and soaring into the realm of infinity. Others may picture rows and rows of silent bodies sitting long into the night trying mightily to transcend normal consciousness and attain some sort of enlightened state that will immediately solve all their earthly problems.

The difficulty with these scenarios is that while meditation *can* contain some of these aspects, at its core it is simple, direct, and easy to learn and make a part of one's everyday life. That said, let me also say that for many people, meditation can be the most difficult, painful, and challenging practice of their lives. It can raise issues that have been buried so deep that they have been successfully ignored for a lifetime. It can bring one to the very brink of one's sanity or it can bore one to tears.

On the other hand, meditation, practiced correctly and regularly in the way that is most appropriate for each individual, can open doorways into worlds that we can only imagine. It can open lines of communication to the world of helping and healing spirits and can bring one closer to whatever one's idea of God or Dao or the Great Mystery is. Daoist meditation is often called "Embracing the One" or "Returning to the Source." There is much about it that is mystical and may at first seem hard to understand for the beginner. Meditation can also allow one greater awareness of one's bodily condition or energetic state, as well as allow greater insight into one's emotional terrain.

Many people in the West have a very difficult time sitting still. They fidget, stretch, make noises, sway back and forth, and change their posture over and over. Unfortunately, it is impossible to attain inner stillness without first attaining outer stillness. The very first prerequisite for attaining the deep levels of inner stillness and quietude needed for deep meditation work is that one can sit still with the spine straight for at least twenty minutes at a time. Because this is so difficult for many beginners, the best thing to do is start with a shorter amount of time—say five minutes. After a while, you can extend that period until you can sit for twenty to thirty minutes in a stretch without having to change your posture or move around. Twenty or thirty minutes is sufficient for most people. If your goal is to heal a serious health problem or to become an "immortal," then much longer periods of sitting will be necessary.

It is very important to keep the spine erect and straight: not at attention, but as if there were a string pulling you up from the top of your head, from the *baihui* pressure point at the center of the crown (in yoga, called the "crown chakra"), while pulling in your chin slightly. It is important that one does not slump or fidget, but it is equally important that one does not hold one's body too stiffly. One way to avoid this is to always have a gentle smile on your face. Have you ever seen a statue or picture of the Buddha who was not smiling? This will help your meditation from becoming too solemn a practice.

As my teacher Hua-Ching Ni says,

> If your attitude towards meditation is too tight and you sit solemnly and stiffly, you will nourish and increase this overly serious and unpleasant aspect of your practice, and this will become the sour fruit you bear. If, on the other hand, you sit with genuine joy, the world sings to you; the pores and cells of the breeze dance for you.[3]

Indeed, just the art of aligning one's body and sitting quietly for any amount of time will have positive benefits. Whether you are able to still the monkey mind or not, you will still get great benefit from simply sitting in meditation in an aware and relaxed manner.

Daoist meditation is a little different from many other types of Eastern meditation. It does not work solely with the mind, although that is a component of Daoist meditation. It is not just a relaxation practice, though it also has that function. It is not simply a quest for a higher state of consciousness but seeks to balance mind, body, and spirit into one unified field. It utilizes the mind, body, and spirit as well as the life-force energy that animates all living things, which in Chinese is called *qi* (pronounced "chee").

In Daoist energy meditation practices, we direct qi to various organs and through various channels or meridians to facilitate healing, greater vitality, and a long and healthy life. The practices also dissolve areas of "stuck" qi, which can cause anything from pain to tumors. Meditators learn to breathe deeply from the belly, thereby exercising the diaphragm muscle and massaging the digestive organs. They also learn to breathe into the lower and upper back, massaging the kidneys and the heart.

To someone on the outside it looks as though the meditator is just sitting quietly and breathing deeply. But on the inside, they may be moving energy (qi) up the back channel (*du mai*) and then down the front channel (*ren mai*) in what is called "the small heavenly orbit" (*xiao zhou tian*), or they may be sending qi into various organ systems. They may be breathing not just from the front but with the back as well, feeling their whole body expanding and contracting.

The effects of a regular meditation practice are both internal and external. As practitioners begin to relax into their practice, they will not only feel different; they will also *look* different. Worry lines and wrinkles begin to relax and disappear, and their body, especially the spine, begins to realign itself and their posture changes. The ability to deal with life's challenges and pressures improves dramatically as one's entire disposition changes. Also, a greater sense of clarity, both emotional and psychological, begins to suffuse one's being.

Daoist meditation can also quiet the monkey mind, that part of the brain that never shuts off but runs and jumps from one thought to another like an excited monkey. Another term for Daoist meditation practice is "taming the wild horse." Like a static-ridden radio, our minds are often so full of outside noise that we rarely get to hear that still, small voice within that can give us so much information and guidance from our higher selves, or Dao nature. Just taking a few moments a day to tone down the static and neutralize its effects can bring us serenity of spirit and open pathways of communication from the spirit world.

When we practice this way, our mind becomes both serene (*qing*) and calm (*jing*). Sometimes this state of serenity and calmness is referred to as the naturalness of empty nothingness (*xuwu ziran*), which describes the level of calmness and serenity needed for deep spiritual practice.

Meditation is also referred to as insight practice. By turning our gaze inward, we can illuminate those dark areas of sickness, pain, and emotional turmoil that often run (and ruin) our lives. By gently circulating the golden light within us, we can reach that enlightened state in which our problems do not have as much weight as they did, and we can make decisions from a calm, clear, and balanced state.

Another major difference in Daoist-style meditation practice is that we utilize sitting, lying down, standing, and even moving meditation techniques. To be able to maintain the meditative state while moving is a very valuable and powerful experience that can help bring the meditative state into one's daily life. Many people are familiar with the slow, graceful moves of taiji or qigong. This is called "stillness in movement" and is an important part of Daoist practice. If we can find that point of stillness within our movement, it will be easier for us to bring the meditative state, and all the benefits that come from it, into our daily lives.

The foremost concern of the Daoist is to go with the flow of nature, not expending too much energy and ending up depleted, and not doing anything that is unnatural for the individual. In Chinese this is called *wu wei*, sometimes translated as "not doing." What it really means is being so sensitive to the moment that one is able to do just the right thing at the right time, which may include doing nothing! The important thing is not to overdo anything, including meditation. One of my teachers once told me that too much meditation will make your teeth fall out!

What I understood him to mean is that not moving for too long a time will make our energy or qi stagnate in our lower body, causing all kinds of circulatory disturbances. We are already seeing this happen in the modern world. People sit in front of computers all day, only to go home and sit in front of the television. Of course, the fact that they stuff themselves with high-carbohydrate, low-nutrition foods at the same time only makes things worse and is causing higher rates of diabetes and heart disease.

Another aspect of Daoist meditation is internal alchemy practice, *neidan*. Briefly, internal alchemy is concerned with the mixing and refining of internal energies in order to reach deeper states of health and spiritual cultivation. These are referred to in ancient Daoist texts as "immortality practices."

By learning how to harmonize and strengthen the physical, mental, and energetic layers of our body, we not only revitalize our system but gain deeper spiritual awareness and understanding that will, in turn, allow us to be examples to others.

Daoists do not proselytize, they do not sermonize, and they do not seek to convert others. Instead, they believe that being a good example of a healthy, spiritually realized person is the best way to help the world. We all learn at our own pace, in our own time, and in our own fashion. That is why there are so many different types of practices in Daoism and why there is no one practice that is right for everyone. Zhuangzi says, "We cannot see our reflection in running water, only in still water. Only a person who has attained inner stillness is able to still the minds of others."[4]

There are many reasons to begin a meditation practice, from cutting down the stress in your life to seeking immortality. Human beings have always meditated. The oldest cultures, including Indian and Chinese, have utilized various meditation practices to maintain health, stamina, and vitality, as well as to commune with the source of all life, or what the Chinese call Dao.

All these are valid reasons to begin or maintain a meditation practice. The trick, of course, is to be able to bring the meditative state, or the fruits thereof, into the rest of your life. The more you can erase the line between your meditation or spiritual practices and the rest of your life, the better. The more you integrate meditation into your life, the more whole, balanced, harmonious, healthy, insightful, and spiritually aware you will be.

Of course, Daoists, rooted in Chinese culture, are also very practical about their practice. If one is sick, unbalanced, ungrounded, or emotionally confused, it is very difficult to enter the deep spiritual realms of immortality practices. Thus they developed health practices like taiji, *dao-in* (Daoist yoga), and qigong—practices to help the students of the Way stay as strong, healthy, and clear-minded as possible. In this way they were better able to keep up with life's demands and to delve deeply into the meditation practices that were necessary for the Daoist adept.

But if one is interested in spiritually evolving or attaining Dao, one must pay attention to the internal cultivation practices as well as the movement forms. We must remember that the qigong or movement forms are there to support our spiritual practice, much of which consists of stillness or meditation practice.

Laozi gives us this advice on meditation:

Can you hold the body and spirit as one?
Can you avoid their separation?
Concentrating your qi
and becoming pliant,
can you become like a
newborn baby?
Clearing your mind and
contemplating the profound,
can you remain unflawed?[5]

Daoists believe in learning from nature, both external and internal. Ancient Daoists spent a lot of time studying nature around them. They watched how some animals comport themselves to rest by turning in circles before lying down, how certain birds stand on one leg with the other leg raised to seal up the lower opening, and how other animals curl up to close off various openings, thereby stopping any energy leakage. They noticed which plants animals ate when they were sick or injured.

They observed the slow passing of each season, of day into night, and the interplay between light and dark. They experimented on themselves with various breathing practices and with sitting and even lying down meditation postures. Over thousands of years of experimentation, they came up with various practices that have stood the test of time. They found ways to open the doorways between worlds, to extend life, and to heal the deep layers of trauma that we as humans have accumulated through lifetimes.

As in ancient days, the best teacher is still nature, if one has the eyes to see. But even that can take training and practice. The next best teacher is life itself, but one must be able to look with a gaze of objectivity and introspection, something not all of us have been trained to do. The best teacher after that is another person, a teacher of meditation or qigong. There are some things that you can receive from another person that you can never get from a book or a video, especially if that person is a gifted teacher. After that, knowledge can come from books, podcasts, and videos.

Depending on how much you put into it, Daoist meditation can effectively change or, at the very least, enhance your life. For those with experience in other forms of meditation, it can open new areas of experience and vision. Daoist meditation can give you greater clarity, both emotionally and mentally, a stronger sense of groundedness in your energy body, and some valuable tools for exploring the inner space of your psyche, spirit, and energetic being.

Last of all, Daoist meditation is not necessarily connected to a religious format. In other words, it is not necessary to convert to Daoism to practice Daoist meditation. The benefits of Daoist meditation can be experienced by anyone, regardless of religious persuasion. All it takes is the willingness to relax, to be open to change, and to experience oneself as an energetic as well as a spiritual being.

Laozi says,

Allow yourself to become empty.
Abide in stillness.
The ten thousand beings rise and flourish

while the sage watches their return.
Though all beings exist in profusion,
they all end up returning to their source.
Returning to their source is called "tranquility."
This is called "returning to their original nature."
Original nature is called "constant renewal."
To understand constant renewal is called "illumination."[6]

Most of what we know of today as qigong practices were originally developed as aids to meditation. The earliest form of qigong that we know of is dao-in. Dao-in practices, which date back to the Han dynasty (206 B.C.E.–220 C.E.), were created to lead qi into its proper channels with various stretching, twisting, and self-massage movements.

Yang sheng, or "nourishing life practices," is another ancient term for what today we call qigong, dietary teachings, herbal medicine, and meditation, among other practices. The ancient Daoist sages saw our body as the storehouse of our inner nature. They taught that we must take care of our body in order to have a good place for our spirit to dwell. In this way, our physical/energetic practice provides a foundation for our spiritual cultivation.

It is important not to neglect our stillness practice if we are to fully enjoy the benefits of our movement practice. Like yin and yang, both movement and stillness are important to our overall cultivation of health and well-being. Daoists believe that it is important to keep a balance between movement and stillness. Too much movement will exhaust one's qi, while excessive sitting will cause stagnation in the body.

The key here is to not abandon one for the other but to experiment and see what the proper balance is for your own cultivation.

Like yin within yang, or stillness within movement, that place of serene stillness in our meditation practice gives birth to that subtle and mysterious movement within the stillness. That movement brings us into greater harmony, greater awareness, and greater experience of the eternal and ever-evolving Dao.

2

Why Daoism?

When the thinking mind can go no further,
when language comes to an end, when nothing can
be described, then you can see the true Tao.[7]

—HUA-CHING NI

TODAY WE LIVE IN A WORLD rife with problems of every kind—environmental, political, economic, religious, and interpersonal. Everywhere we look we see pain, suffering, and degradation. Many people feel cut off, alone, unneeded, and inconsequential. The homeless are everywhere, even in the once-proud United States, staring out at us with sad, desperate eyes. The delicate ecological balance of our planet seems hopelessly upset. The threat of nuclear annihilation only serves to distract us from fears of new plagues, terrorist attacks, and the ever-growing number of chronic illnesses that seem to elude our finest medical minds.

What can Daoism, a five-thousand-year-old philosophy of ancient China, have to offer at this crucial time? Today's problems are real, concrete, and seemingly irresolvable. They call for something besides fantasies and visions, something that can be applied to everyday life with its everyday problems. Daoism offers not a way out but a way through. Its solutions are real, concrete, and eminently applicable, regardless of one's race, religion, or gender. Although Daoists have been called dreamy-eyed mystics, nothing could be further from the truth. What the ancient masters learned through countless years of observation and practice can be just as useful today as it was in the time of the Yellow Emperor,[8] if not more so.

The modern world bombards us on every side with sensory, emotional, and psychological impressions. We often feel alone and cut off from our foundations, both spiritually and emotionally. For many of us, reality consists of spoon-size treatments of other people's lives, fed to us in a steady diet by newspapers, radio, and especially television, where everyone's life problems are solved in a half-hour segment that includes commercials. We feel disappointed and inferior if we are not able to work the same magic with our own problems.

Many Westerners, impressed by the culture and history of the East, are drawn to its thought, art, music, food, medicine, and philosophies. But Daoism is not just some ancient, foreign, mystical path. In truth, it is transcultural, nonsexist, practical, and scientific. Its practices work on many levels—physical, emotional, psychological, and spiritual. It can be applied to political action, environmental concerns, economic interests, emotional clearing, health problems, business enterprises, psychological balance, sexuality, and spiritual fulfillment. It works well for highly individualized Westerners and can be approached on any level, from the rank beginner to the evolved aspirant.

As the wonderful John Blofeld puts it,

> If curious rock-formations remind you of strange animals in the throes of creation; if the blossom of the crab-apple or winter-plum bears a message that goes beyond mere prettiness; if water tumbling into a mountain pool fills you with inexplicable rapture; if walking in the rain makes you long to dance and sing; if a vista of rocks, pine trees and purple hills seems to hint at what the poet Li T'ai-po calls "another universe, a realm of Immortals," then you have the makings of a Taoist.[9]

Why does Daoism affect people like this? Perhaps it has something to do with the Daoist emphasis on naturalness and respect for the cycles of change, both within and without. Daoism's teachings of wu wei (not overdoing), the watercourse way (following the current of natural phenomena), and the concept of yin/yang offer something in their simplicity that many Western religions lack.

Many of the beliefs and practices of Daoism were already long established when Laozi wrote the *Daodejing*. Daoism's original ideas—such as wu wei, the watercourse way, meditation (described numerous times in the *Daodejing*), not exalting the high over the low, taking it one step at a time (a famous passage from Laozi), being flexible (like the young plant), not building up riches, letting go of intellectual knowledge, the soft overcoming the hard, keeping quiet about one's attainments, being humble, leading from behind, not struggling, not arguing, not being afraid of death—are all contained in the early writings of Laozi, Zhuang, and Liehzi (Lieh Tzu). They originated in the ancient shamanic roots (*wu*) of Chinese civilization. For centuries Daoism was an informal way of life, a way followed by peasant, farmer, gentleman philosopher, and artist. It was a way of deep reflection and of learning from nature. Followers of the Way studied the stars in the heavens and the energy that lies deep within the earth (*feng shui*). They meditated on the energy flow within their own bodies and mapped out the roads and paths it traveled on.

Daoism is a belief in life, a belief in the glorious procession of each unfolding moment. It is a deeply spiritual way of life, involving introspection, balance, emotional and spiritual independence and responsibility, and a deep awareness and connection to the Earth and all other life forms. It gives us an understanding of how energy works in the body and how to treat illness in a safe, noninvasive way, while teaching practical ways of maintaining health and avoiding disease and discomfort. Daoist meditation techniques help the practitioner enter deeper or more expansive levels of wakefulness and inner strength. But most of all, it is a simple, natural, practical way of being in our bodies and our psyches and sharing that way of being with all other life-forms we encounter.

The original "Daoists" often ended up in the mountains, where they could live close to heaven and nature and far away from the emperor. Indeed, the word for sage in Chinese is *zhenren,* a combination of the characters for person and mountain. It was in the mountains that they could find a combination of good qi (vital energy) as well as good *de* (spiritual vitality) that they needed for their cultivation practices. It also helped that they were far away from the tawdry affairs of a society that did not always appreciate those who trod their own path.

The path of Dao is one that grounds us in our bodies and roots us in the earth while opening us to the healing energy of the heavens. It is a path of joy and creativity and deep belly laughter. It is a path that reminds us, constantly and deeply, of our place in the world and of our connection to all other life forms on this earth, "the ten thousand beings" (*wan wu*).

Dao is at once the universal pageant of the constellations and the budding of each new leaf in the spring. It is the constant round of life and death and all that falls between. It resides in us as we reside in it. It is the source as well as the end of our being. It neither judges nor condemns but continually blesses, in all moments, an unending cycle of change and renewal.

The path of Daoism that we will be exploring in this book is not an "ism." It is also not an ideology or a New Age movement. It is a *living philosophy*. It is a way of thinking, a way of looking at life, a way of being—being *with* change rather than *against* it. Life is made up of cycles, say the Daoists, cycle upon cycle. The only constant is change. Change is inescapable. We have no control over it. The only thing we have control over is our own responses to the changes life has to offer. For really, what else *can* we do?

Laozi says,

Yield and become whole.
Bend and become straight.

Empty yourself and become filled.
Grow old yet become renewed.
Have little yet acquire much.
Become whole and you will be restored to Dao.[10]

Laozi describes a Daoist as one who sees simplicity in the complicated and achieves greatness in little things. He or she is dedicated to discovering the dance of the cosmos in the passing of each season as well as the passing of each precious moment in our lives. Laozi calls this person a sage (*zhenren*).

3

Daoist Principles to Enhance Your Meditation Practice

HERE ARE A FEW of the most important principles in Daoism that have a direct influence on our meditation experience. While it can be difficult to separate these major principles in Daoist teaching, we will go over each one on its own.

The first one is wu wei (pronounced "oo way"). *Wu wei* translates as "not doing," "not overdoing," or "not overextending." It is not about doing nothing, which is how some Westerners have translated it. It is about doing the right thing at the right time, with the least amount of effort. Sometimes it is referred to as "effortless effort."

Wu wei can also mean not overeating, not overexercising, or even not overthinking. By overeating we fill our stomach with so much food that it cannot deal with it all and our digestive process is thereby slowed down, which can cause all sorts of health problems. By not overexercising, we do not exhaust our body. Daoists usually practice very gentle kinds of exercise, such as taiji and qigong. Walking is also encouraged. If you are a person who needs more physical exercise, there are various martial arts (*wushu*) that you can practice.

Thinking too much or overthinking every little thing can also get in the way of emotional and even spiritual happiness. This is where Daoist meditation comes in. By quieting our mind and heart (the same thing in Chinese thought) we can allow our parasympathetic nervous system to calm down, our heart rate to slow down, and things like stress and emotional turmoil to clear up, thereby inducing a feeling of calmness and peace.

The next important principle is *manzou*, or "go slowly." This means to approach your life in a natural and graceful way, not allowing yourself to rush into things, even meditation. When we meditate, we breathe slowly and deeply. If we started by breathing too quickly or hyperventilating, our meditation session would not go well. This is about moving slowly (as in taiji practice), eating slowly, speaking slowly (so that others can really hear what we are saying), and listening slowly (so that we can really hear what others are saying).

Nowadays in China, when you say goodbye to someone you say "Zaijian," or "Goodbye." But in the old days when you said goodbye to someone, especially if they were the ones leaving, you would say "Manzou," or "Go slowly away from me." If we are rushing through our days at a frenetic pace, even our meditation practice will take on that frenetic energy, and our experience will be much less powerful. Also, trying to accomplish too much too fast in our meditation practice can have a negative effect. It is better to just go slowly and establish a strong energetic/spiritual foundation and then build from there. This is why we have such an emphasis on working with the lower *dantian,* located in our lower abdomen, especially when we first begin practicing Daoist energy meditation.

Another important Daoist principle is the watercourse way or going with the flow. This is about learning how to apply wu wei to our own flow of life as well as the flow of life around us. It may be difficult sometimes to ascertain just what is the flow in any given moment. One of the things that can help with this is the principle of manzou. It will be much easier to realize just what the flow is in any situation if we are not moving too fast. If we are moving too fast or are trying to accomplish too much in our meditation practice, we are going against the flow.

Of course, the flow is changing or transforming all the time. What works in one instance may not work in another. This is why we need to be able to slow down enough to feel what is right each time. Like yin/yang, the situation can often be very fluid, and if we are able to be fluid in our own bodies and being, we can go *with* the flow rather than *against* it.

Another great quality about water is that it is very adaptable. If we put it into a round container, it becomes round. If we put it into a square container, it becomes square. The idea is to be as adaptable as we can so that whatever situation or container we find ourselves in, we can adapt to it and thus avoid causing ourselves pain.

The next principle is *pu,* or what is often called "the uncarved block"—the simple block of wood before the carver starts working on it. It is also about not doing anything that is not in our nature or the greater nature of the world around us.

At first it may be difficult to learn just what *is* our true nature. We have all become so layered over with things that have been forced on us by family, education, religion, politics, and so on that we have no idea who we authentically are under all those layers. But doing these Daoist cultivation practices will allow us to shed these layers, one by one, so that we can shine forth as the true, beautiful, and natural being that we are! Some people are naturally more yin in their nature. Others are more yang. But if we try to twist ourselves around so that we can be like other people, this will cause us pain and suffering. It's better to just naturally be who you are. This doesn't mean that we can't grow and change. But it is best to do it in a slow, natural, wu wei way.

Which brings us to the next important principle: flexibility. Laozi tells us that when the plant is young it is very juicy and flexible, but when it is old it becomes dry and brittle and breaks easily. This is what happens for many people as well. As they become older they get set in their ways and are no longer open to new things, new ideas, new travels, or even new food. Of course, it is also important to age gracefully in our bodies. If we don't exercise in a joyful way, if we don't eat a good diet and don't ever stretch our bodies, we will begin to dry up and become brittle and break, just like that dried-up plant.

Most important, though, is that we do not become dry and brittle in our minds. What we are going for in this Daoist lifestyle is to live in a groove instead of a rut. There is a big difference between experiencing our lives as a graceful dance and being stuck in a rut of our own making.

Zhuangzi tells us that blindness and deafness not only afflict people physically but also exist in the minds and attitudes of people. It's better to keep an open mind and heart, to learn and experience life as an adventure to be lived and loved, than to hide our hearts away from the world.

Of course, there are other important principles in living a life of free and easy wandering, and we will be going over them in this meditation journey I am sharing with you.

4

Stillness Meditation

Allow yourself to become empty.
Abide in stillness.[11]

—*DAODEJING*

Do not yearn for beautiful meditation experiences.
Just sit and let the mind clear itself.
Sit and let the body become calm.[12]

—STUART ALVE OLSEN

STILLNESS MEDITATION is called by various names, such as "sitting and forgetting" (*zuowang*), "tranquility practice," "abiding in stillness," and "holding to the one" (*zhou yi*). This is the kind of practice that most people think of when they become interested in meditation. But as you will see in this book, it is just one of a number of meditation styles in the Daoist tradition.

Stillness meditation is not necessarily about going into a trance state, though that may happen. It is more like mud settling to the bottom of a glass of water, as the *Daodejing* famously describes it. When our mind is too full and scattered, it is like a glass of water mixed with dirt or mud. If we continue to shake the glass, the dirt swirls around in the water, making it impossible to see through. But if we stop shaking the glass and quiet our madly running monkey mind, the mud will settle to the bottom of the glass, allowing the water, and our spirit, to become clear.

In this meditation we will be working with our lower dantian, located three inches behind our navel. The term *dantian* means "field of medicine" or "field of elixir." It is an important energy center in our body. There are three dantians: the lower dantian; the middle dantian, in the center of the chest and corresponding to the heart center; and the upper dantian, located between our eyebrows and an inch or so inside our forehead, and corresponding to the celestial or heavenly eye (*tian mu*). In other chapters we will be working with both the middle and the upper dantian.

The middle dantian is called "the crimson palace" (*jiang gong*) in Daoist energetic practices (see chapter 27). It is a much smaller area than the lower dantian. It is sometimes referred to as "the yellow court" (*huangting*) or "the mysterious female" (*xuanpin*). It is also known as the seat of our *shen*, or indwelling spirit.

Our upper dantian is called "the hall of light" (tian mu) (see chapter 25). It is also called the celestial eye or third eye. This area is connected to our pineal gland, a tiny gland in our brain that is said to be associated with psychic abilities.

Our lower dantian also corresponds to when we were in our mother's womb and being fed from her through our umbilical cord. The Daoists say that at this point, we are not really living in the material world as such but are still very connected with what they call the pre-heaven state. It is only when our umbilical cord is cut that we enter the post-heaven state.

We need to create our own womb in our energetic body. This is true for males as well as females. A lot of the lower dantian practices are to create that energetic womb so that we can give birth to our new, more spiritual self, often called "the golden embryo" (*shengtai*) in Daoist internal alchemy practice. This is a very important area of our energetic anatomy. When we are in our mother's womb, we get all our nutrition, as well as breath, through our umbilical cord, which is connected to our navel. Most people think nothing of having a belly button and believe it has no use after we are born. But in Daoist practice, it is the beginning or gateway into our lower dantian. Unlike the very small acupuncture points, the dantian, and especially the lower dantian, are much larger fields.

In any case, by focusing our mind and our breath on our lower dantian, we begin to build an energetic foundation for our meditation practice. It is like building a strong foundation before raising the walls of a building. In ancient woodcut illustrations in books on internal alchemy, practitioners are often shown with a cauldron in their lower abdomen. The cauldron represents the place where we mix the different kinds of qi or medicine in order to create a powerful type of healing.

Another important thing about stillness meditation, and meditation in general, is that it helps us to focus. Our modern information-age society teaches us the opposite and weakens our ability to focus on anything for more than a few minutes (or less). Our ability to go deeply into the meditation state is directly conditioned on our ability to concentrate both our attention and our qi, or our mind and our body. If our attention span is too short and our ability to focus the same, then our meditation practice will be shallow and unproductive.

But the beauty of meditation practice is that, when done correctly and consistently, our ability to concentrate and focus will be strengthened. So don't worry if you can keep your focus for only a few minutes at a time. The more consistent your practice, the stronger your ability to focus will be, even in other areas of your life.

Another important principle is that your meditation life and your active life need to be experienced as one thing, not two. Your waking and dreaming life are also one thing, not two. Your spiritual life and your mundane life need to be aligned so that you experience them as one. This is a very important teaching. If you are able to balance yourself this way, you are one with Dao, or Source.

If you find yourself nodding off while meditating, try getting up and doing some moving meditation practice, such as taiji or qigong, for a few minutes. Rubbing your palms up and down your face can also help. You can also do a simple qigong practice called "beating the heavenly drum" (*ming tian gu*). This is done by cupping your ears with your palms, shutting out all sound. Then, with your first finger on top of your middle finger, flick your first finger over the base of your skull, making a bright, booming sound in your ear. Do this thirty-six times. This will wake you up by vibrating the brain fluid in your skull.

You can do these practices whenever you need to give yourself a little wake-up after long hours at the computer or first thing in the morning. It is not recommended to do it too much at night, as it can bring more qi or energy to your head, which might interfere with your sleep. It is ideal to spend at least twenty minutes in meditation, at least once a day. Often, though, we spend the first five minutes relaxing, the next five trying to focus our mind, the next five on slowing our thought processes, and only during the last five minutes may we touch on a deep meditation state.

The length of your meditation is not as important as the depth of your focus. Daoists are very flexible. If you have more time one day for meditation, do it longer. If on another day you have less time, do it for a shorter time. Practicing meditation regularly will allow you to develop meditation muscles. Just as doing physical exercise will build stronger muscles in your body, meditation muscles will allow you to drop down into deep meditation very quickly and easily. This is why the twenty-minute suggestion is important. There are many meditation teachers and courses out there that say all you need to do is five minutes a day, but unless you are highly experienced and can actually drop down into deep meditation for those five minutes, it would be better to put a little more time into it.

The more you practice meditation the stronger your meditation muscles will be. Not having a regular and dedicated practice is like wanting to be stronger physically but not doing any muscle training. Practicing meditation is a little like depositing money in the bank. Even if it is just a small amount, by doing it regularly it adds up. The important thing is not to stress about it. By putting ourselves into a stressful state about our relaxation practice we are defeating our own practice!

Try to include as many mini-meditations during the day as you can. If you are working on a computer, take a few moments every once in a while to close your eyes, slow your breath, and relax your mind. If you are traveling as a passenger, use the time to close your eyes, slow down your breathing, and drop into your lower dantian.

Daoist masters also tell us not to get so caught up in our meditation that we neglect the rest of our lives. Another term for meditation in Daoism is *zuowang*, or "sitting and forgetting." This kind of forgetting is very different than normal forgetting. In this case what we are forgetting is our ties to the material world or our ever-changing emotional state. Sometimes this kind of meditation is called "abiding in stillness" and is the precursor to zazen, or Zen sitting meditation.

Stillness meditation is also called "fasting of the mind," as described in this passage from Zhuangzi:

> You must center your heart/mind in perfect harmony. . . . Do not listen with your ears but with your heart/mind. Do not listen with your heart/mind but with your vital energy [qi]. Hearing stops with the ears, thoughts and ideas stop with the mind. Your [qi] or vital energy though resides in stillness and is open and receptive to all things.

> True knowledge or [D]ao resides in stillness and emptiness and to attain this emptiness one must use the fasting of the mind.[13]

It is when we sit in stillness that we can forget our ego and our many opinions and judgments that we habitually use to impose order on our world. The Daoists say let go of these opinions and judgments and let your true Dao self emerge. Remember, when coming out of a deep meditation it is important not to jump into the usual activities too suddenly. You may be in a very sensitive state, and having to deal with any kind of stress right away can undo all the good work you just did.

Of course, as I am sure you have heard before, it is crucial to be able to take this calm and centered state into the rest of our lives. It does us no good at all if we are able to reach states of deep relaxation and calmness when in meditation but lose it once we re-enter the world. There is a certain kind of power that is gained by spending time in stillness. It is also by cultivating stillness and centeredness in the midst of activity that we bring ourselves to the real depths of the practice.

True power comes from our deep connection to heaven, earth, and our own eternal being, Dao. Daoist meditation is not just some kind of relaxation therapy. It creates a way to connect with our own powerful inner being.

Stillness Meditation

TO BEGIN, sit on the floor with a cushion under you, or else sit on a chair with your feet flat on the floor. Sitting cross-legged is fine if that is best for your body, as is a half lotus posture, where our left leg is up on our right thigh. If you are young or very flexible, the full lotus (where both legs are placed on the opposite thigh) is great because it gives you a nice balance point between your knees and your spine. You can also just sit cross-legged if that is better for your body. You can also do this type of meditation lying down or sitting on a chair if you have mobility issues.

Keep your spine straight, yet not stiff. Feel your head as being suspended from above by a silken thread. Sitting up straight when doing sitting meditation or qigong is very important. It is very difficult for the qi or energy to flow through your body if you are slumped over. You should not be sitting at attention but just in a relaxed state of being—upright in body and in mind.

- Take three deep cleansing breaths, exhaling fully and forcefully through the nose.
- Close your eyes. This is called "dropping the curtain" in Daoist practice and will make it easier to look within. We take in so much information of the world through our eyes that it is good to take a rest from that and spend some time exploring our inner world.

- Next, place the tip of your tongue to your upper palate. This links up the two major energy channels in your body, the du mai that runs up our back, and the ren mai that runs down our front.
- Close your mouth and breathe through your nose. Inhale slowly, deeply, and gently. Let your focus be on your breath as it enters and leaves your body.

  By resting your mind on your breath, you will be able to create a balance between oblivion and distraction—always a challenge, especially in the beginning. This is where you untie the knots in your mind and enter the timeless time for a while. Don't worry about what went on before you began meditating, and don't worry about what will go on after. Leave your worries and concerns behind as you follow your breath in and out.
- Put your focus on your lower abdomen. As you breathe in, feel your abdomen expand; and as you exhale, feel it contract. When you inhale, you should feel your lower abdomen expanding to the front, the sides, and the back. If you are sitting up against the back of a chair or a wall, you should feel your back pushing into the chair or wall. This kind of lower-dantian breathing is also referred to as "natural breathing."

  As you begin to breathe in this way, even if it is only when you are meditating, you will notice that your breathing patterns change. This very calming, nurturing, and energizing form of breathing can have great effects throughout the rest of your life. When we go into a "fight or flight" mode, our breathing stops or becomes very shallow. Many people breathe this way all the time, meaning they are constantly in a hypervigilant mode, causing great stress to their nervous systems.

As you breathe, each inhale leads to an exhale, and each exhale leads to an inhale. They are not two different things but one. The act of filling with air and qi and the act of breathing out air and qi is one thing only, not two things.

- Whether you are doing special energetic practices or just "sitting and forgetting," when your time is up, or when you feel that your sense of inner quietude is beginning to dissolve, bring your palms together in front of your face and rub them briskly together thirty-six times.
- Then place them gently over your eyes and breathe the warmth of your palms (*laogong*) into your eyes, all the way into the center of your brain to your pineal gland, a tiny gland that is a critical part of your endocrine system. Then rub your palms over your face three times to wake yourself up from the meditation.

5

Healing Light Meditation

IN THIS MEDITATION we will be working on filling our body and being with healing light from the sun, moon, and stars—that is, the celestial realm. It is an opportunity to cleanse ourselves of any disease, toxicity, pain, or stress, whether physical, emotional, psychological, or spiritual. I like the practice of visualizing all this leaving your body and psyche as black smoke, thereby making it a very tactile experience.

Healing Light Meditation

- Sit, stand, or lie down, and begin breathing deeply and slowly, your lower abdomen expanding with each inhale and contracting with each exhale, like blowing up a balloon and then letting the air out of it. Be sure to keep the tip of your tongue on the roof of your mouth.
- After a while, feel your back expanding and contracting as well, then the sides of your abdomen. Feel your

lower dantian fill toward the front, the back, and the sides. Feel your sense of center there in the lower dantian.

The lower dantian is also called the cauldron. When we put the attention of our mind (fire) down into our lower dantian (water), alchemy can happen. Your lower dantian is more of an area than a point and is located directly behind your navel at least a third of the way inside your abdomen.

- Feel each breath expanding your whole being and then contracting it. This itself is a powerful practice that can produce feelings of calmness, focus, and power. One of the secrets to a successful meditation session is to smile slightly. You will find that it changes the whole experience if you have a slight smile rather than a serious frown. Many people think of meditation as serious business, and the fruit of their meditation is often bitter. But if you bring a lightness of spirit to your meditation, you will instead enjoy the sweet flowers of your practice.
- Now, in your mind's eye, see yourself surrounded by golden light. This is the healing light of the universe and is a very real thing. Begin to inhale this golden light through your nose. Feel it filling your entire being, going deep to wherever you have pain, disease, toxicity, or stress. Picture it lighting up all the dark places in your body, filling you with light and healing qi.
- After a while, begin to breathe out all the pain, stress,

disease, or toxins on each exhale. See it in your mind's eye as coming out of your body like black smoke, dissipating into the air in front of you.

- Breathe in healing light or qi and breathe out the black smoke for a while. Feel yourself becoming lighter, easier, and more energetically clean. In Daoist practice this is called *tuna*: expelling impure and pathogenic energy from the body. You can also use this practice to release any emotions or mind states that are no longer serving you. Feel them release from your body and psyche and flow out like black smoke.

  Spend some time with this to really dive deeply into the practice. At some point you can stop directing the healing light and just let it enter your body and psyche on its own. The light, or the healing qi, has a kind of intelligence and can enter your body and even your emotional states on its own and just work where it needs to without you directing it with your mind. After breathing in the healing light and exhaling the black smoke, you can then breathe in golden light and exhale golden light as well.

- Feel the healing light or qi fill your whole body and begin releasing it of all concerns and worries. Let your spirit feel light and easy. Feel your whole being fill with light and clear energy. Continue to inhale clear light or qi and exhale the same.
- When you are finished, end the meditation by briskly rubbing your hands together thirty-six times, then place your palms over your eyes and breathe the warmth of

your palms into your eyes. After a few moments, rub them gently up and down your face to bring yourself out of the meditative state.

This practice can also be done lying down if you are too weak to sit. Just make sure you don't drift off to sleep too quickly! Also, if your energy is weak, pay more attention to your inhalation. If you feel your body has too much heat, pay more attention to your exhalation. This also works with high blood pressure. Just be sure that your exhalations are long and slow.

You can keep doing this practice until you feel you are done releasing, harmonizing, and healing all the parts of you that you need help with at this time. You may return to it later when you need to delve a little deeper. You may receive different information about your body or psyche at that time.

Be gentle with yourself when you finish and don't leap into the day's activities too quickly.

6

Grounding/ Rooting Meditation

ONE OF THE MOST important practices in Daoism, especially in qigong practice, is grounding or rooting. By grounding ourselves deep into the living, breathing earth, we can receive healing yin energy up into our body through our *yongquan* pressure point on the balls of our feet (the beginning of the kidney meridian).

In traditional Chinese thought, we humans (*ren*) are the balancing point between heaven (*tian*) and earth (*di*). It is our job to manifest both the heavenly star energy and the earth energy into our own being. In this way, we will be able to share with others what we have learned and what we have become.

When we think of a tree, most of us visualize the trunk growing up into the sky with its branches, leaves, flowers, and perhaps fruit. It is important to remember that there is a whole other part of the tree: Its roots are growing down deep and wide and are sometimes intermingled with those of other trees around it. This root system may even be larger than the above-ground part of the tree. In other words, to really picture a tree we need to visualize both parts.

So what we want to do is to create our own tree, with our trunk, limbs, branches, and leaves growing up toward the life-giving sun as well as our root system digging deep into the equally life-giving earth. If our root system is small or weak, our energy will be small and weak. We will feel ungrounded and easily knocked off-center. But if our root system is strong, we will be able to weather the storms of life and be able to spring back up when knocked down.

Grounding/Rooting Meditation

STAND ON THE EARTH (ideal) or sit on a chair, feet flat on the floor.

- Spend some time doing deep natural breathing. Be sure to breathe slowly, deeply, and gently. Feel your mind begin to quiet down and your breathing become deeper and slower.
- With an intent mind, send roots from the bottom of your feet deep down into the earth, at least three times the length of your body. In your mind's eye, feel and see these roots burrowing down like the roots of a great tree, through all the layers of dirt, rock, and animal burrows, deep into the living, breathing earth. Be sure to send them wide as well as deep. Feel yourself

as a strong tree with roots going deep into the earth. Take some time with this.

- When you feel you have a good connection, draw healing yin energy from the earth up through those roots, through the bottom of your feet, then up to your lower dantian. If you are outside next to trees, you can link your roots up to whatever trees are in your vicinity, which will make the strong wood energy of the trees available to you. Feel your own roots intertwining and communicating with all the other trees in the area, just as the roots of trees actually do.
- Feel your entire body filling with the strong yin energy of the earth, as if drinking through a straw. Feel it as a strong grounding force in your whole body and being. Stand or sit like this for a while, then when you are ready, begin to move or walk around the room, or even better, on the earth, while still feeling grounded and rooted.
- Feel yourself energetically sinking down into the earth, with all your movements coming from that place of deep connection with the earth.

Whether you are doing qigong, taiji, yoga, or just walking on the earth, you will be amazed at how powerful your practice will become!

As an extra level of practice, you can energetically open your baihui pressure point, located on the crown of your head, to receive the yang heavenly energy from the celestial realm. To do this we need to focus on our baihui and breathe into it, imagining this important energy center opening like a flower. One of the ways you can tell that it is working is when you get a feeling on the top of your head like ants are walking on it. But it is important that you do not scratch it, as it will cause the point to close.

- Draw it down energetically through your head and all the way down to your lower dantian.
- Feel it mix there with the earthly energy, filling you up with strong healing qi.

Do this even for a short time each day or especially before you start a meditation, qigong, taiji, or yoga session, and your practice will become much richer and more powerful. Not only that, but your emotions will become more balanced, and your sense of your core self will become stronger and clearer.

When we are ungrounded our practice will not be strong, and we will be more susceptible to the winds of change and more easily knocked off center. Use this grounding practice to become stronger, more emotionally independent, and energetically powerful. By creating a strong sense of being rooted and centered in our lower dantian, whenever life knocks us down, instead of lying there whining we will bounce back up again!

If we plant our roots deeply into the earth, we will also experience ourselves as being firmly planted in Dao. Laozi tells us that whoever is firmly planted in Dao cannot be uprooted. The martial arts, taiji, and qigong teach us to always move from our center. If we are deeply rooted, we can always move from this solid center. If we are not, then any little breeze will knock us down and it will be difficult to get back up again. Another thing to remember is that we will not be able to fly unless we are securely and solidly grounded.

You can also use this grounding practice whenever you find yourself in a tense or stressful situation or mindset. By doing the practice, even for a few minutes, you can pull yourself out of the stress and feel solid and deeply connected with the living, breathing earth. This alone can be of great help in difficult or stressful situations.

7

Sacred Space Meditation

IT IS IMPORTANT to do your meditation or qigong practice away from general traffic so that you can go deep without being disturbed. It's great to practice qigong by the water, in a forest, or on a beach, but anywhere you feel free and open is fine—whether that's in a park in the center of a busy city or in the comfort of your own home.

In spring or summer, or any time the weather is mild, it is best to do it outdoors. Cold or windy days are not recommended for outdoor practice. If you are indoors, it is important not to be in an area where other people are moving through. If you do not have a special area for practice, it is fine to use the living room or a bedroom or even a storeroom, as long as you aren't disturbed.

I actually have a temple in my backyard! (It was a big selling point for me when I bought the house.) But for those of you who do not have a temple in your yard, you can make any space into a sacred space. It is really all about the energy and intent that you bring to it. It is good to have an altar, even a small one, with space for flowers and perhaps images that speak to your heart. It can be a simple image of a saint or goddess to whom you feel connected or a picture of your teacher.

Incense has been used for thousands of years as a pathway to communicate and connect with the spirit world. It is also helpful to induce a feeling of calm and spiritual connection. Something simple like sandalwood or aloeswood (sometimes called agarwood) is best, not anything overly sweet. To offer incense, hold either one or three sticks together and light it. Be careful not to blow it out with your breath; instead, shake it or wave your hand in front of it, as it is considered disrespectful to blow it out with your mouth. Then hold it with two hands and bow three times before putting it into whatever incense holder you are using.

Here is an invocation for offering incense, from my Daoist teacher Hua-Ching Ni:

I cultivate myself and follow the Heavenly way with a lucid mind and subtle energy.
With this incense, I connect my whole being with that of all Divine Immortals.
Incense is burned in this beautiful censer so that I may present my spirit and mind
to the highest realm of universal integration.

Eyes of the divine spirits, gaze upon my heart and reflect my devotion to the truth.
Subtle light of the Divine Immortals, shine upon this earthly altar and make my energy divine and effective.
I request the highest divine energy of the Heaven to respond to me.
I humbly offer this sincere petition through the fragrant vibration of this incense.[14]

Sacred space is also any place where people have done spiritual practices over time, so that the space itself becomes impregnated with spiritual energy (de). Anyone who has visited sacred sites anywhere in the world, such as Machu Picchu, the Wudang Mountains, or Mount Shasta, knows that there is a feeling of majestic calm in such places.

When we visit a historic sacred spot, we can pick up on its inherently powerful qi or energy, and that can enhance our own spiritual practice. In Chan or Zen, this is called "locking eyebrows with the masters." Of course, you can instill that kind of energy in your own sacred space, especially after you have spent some time there. By filling that special space with your own spiritual energy, you will be able to create an area that speaks to you as soon as you enter it. Timeless time is good for your heart and your soul. The more timeless time you spend in your sacred space, the more it will be filled with good qi and good feelings, which will allow you to drop down into deep meditation easily and quickly.

Taking it to another level, you can create a shrine or altar in your own heart. In this way, even when you are traveling and do not have access to your home space, you can connect to the altar in your heart. You can use your imagination to place sacred images that speak to you into this inner altar. Try to impress it with the same feelings that you have with your physical altar. This inner altar lives in your heart, your middle dantian, the home of your shen, or spirit. It is a special place in your body and being.

This inner altar can feel even more powerful and sacred than the outer one. Not only that, but you can carry it with you anywhere you go! You can change the images in your inner altar any time you wish.

8

Moving Meditation

THE AIM OF MOVING MEDITATION—taiji and qigong are two examples—is to maintain, while moving, the feeling of deep stillness that we experience when doing quiet sitting meditation. The practice helps us tune into and stay with that beautiful, peaceful feeling when we are out and about in the world. This is one of the ways that Daoist meditation is unique among meditation traditions.

The ancient Daoist sages described the body as the storehouse of our inner nature. They taught that we must take care of the body so that our spirit has a place to dwell. It is important not to neglect our stillness practice if we are to fully enjoy the benefits of our movement practice. Like yin and yang, both movement and stillness practices are important to our overall cultivation of well-being. At the same time, there is now another level of movement within our stillness practice. That movement brings us into greater harmony, greater awareness, and a greater experience of the eternal, ever-evolving Dao and our place in it.

Here is a mantra I learned from one of my teachers that you can do at the start of your moving or standing practice.

You can use both the English and the Chinese or either one. It is a good way to set a tone or field for your practice to flow in. Stand with your feet shoulder-width apart and repeat these simple phrases either aloud or silently.

> Standing with my head in Heaven and my feet on Earth (*Ding tian li di*).
> Relaxed and natural (*Song jing zi ran*).
> In harmony with the universe (*Ren he yu zhou*).
> I am a channel between Heaven and Earth (*Tian di tong guan*).

Here is a simple yet powerful moving meditation from the Wudang Mountains that have been sacred to Daoists for many hundreds of years. It's from the great spiraling dragon qigong form taught there.

Moving Meditation

STAND WITH YOUR FEET shoulder-width apart and facing east, the direction of the sunrise.

- Root deeply into the earth for at least nine breaths.
- Open your baihui point at the top of the head to receive celestial qi for at least nine breaths.
- Now imagine a bright, full moon sitting just above your head, full of healing yin qi.

- Embrace the full yin moon by circling your arms in a medium-sized circle like you are opening your arms to embrace someone, though a little bigger. Exhale the "Ah!" mantra (sort of like a happy sigh).
- Now picture a bright yang sun shining down on you.
- Embrace the yang sun by circling your arms in a much larger circle. Exhale a "Wow!" mantra (a more excited sound and feeling here).
- Do these two movements three to nine times (or more if you like).

Another way to do this practice is to turn and face each direction—east, west, north, and south—and do the movements in each direction.

- Begin by facing east and say, "Green Dragon, lead me forward."
- Then turn right to face the south and say, "Red Phoenix, guard me from above."
- Turn right again to face the west and say, "White Tiger, protect me from behind."
- Then turn right one more time, facing north, and say, "Black Turtle, protect me from below."[15]
- To end, hold the palms over the lower dantian and breathe deeply at least nine times. Men put the right palm over the left, and women put the left palm over the right. Now circle your palms over the lower dantian nine times counterclockwise and nine times clockwise.
- Lastly, bow to the moon, the sun, and the earth.

Here's another simple qigong practice you can do.

Gathering Qi from the Earth and the Sun

STAND WITH YOUR FEET as wide apart as your shoulders.

- Ground yourself by sending roots down into the earth at least three times the length of your body.
- Bring your palms in front of your lower dantian, with palms facing each other.
- In your mind's eye, see a ball of qi, about the size of a soccer ball, between your hands.
- Bring your palms together, then apart, then together again, inhaling when you move your palms away from each other and exhaling as you bring them together until you feel some sort of substance between your hands—a sensation of pressure in your palms as if there was indeed an invisible soccer ball between them. The pressure points in your palms are called *laogong* and are very potent healing points. This practice fills your laogong pressure points that fill your palms with healing qi.
- Now bring your arms down to your sides, palms facing up. Circle your arms out from your sides as you bend your knees, sinking down toward the earth.
- Gather yin qi up from the earth with a scooping motion of your arms. Bring your arms up, palms fac-

ing the heavens, straight in front of you, all the way up to the third-eye level.

- Then turn your palms down and guide the yin earth qi down through the central channel (*chong mai*) that goes from the top of your head down through the very center of your body to your lower dantian.
- Do this nine times, then stand as before.
- Now bring your arms out to the side in a bigger circle, gathering yang qi from above—from the sun, the stars, and the heavens. Bring your hands together over your head (at the baihui pressure point) and guide the qi down your central channel once again, palms down, to your lower dantian. Do this nine times. An important thing about guiding the qi through your central channel is that it does not just pour down like a faucet but actually moves in a spiraling motion.
- Allow yourself to really feel the connection to the earth from the bottom of your feet (the yongquan point) and to the sun and stars from the top of your head (the baihui point). Feel the strong energy of the earth and the sun and stars come into your body as you gather from below and from above. Feel that strong energy moving down through the very center of your body, filling your dantian with healing qi.
- When you are finished, place your hands over your lower dantian, palm over palm, and breathe into this center for at least nine deep breaths. Circle your palms slowly over your dantian, nine times in one direction and then nine times in the other.

Of course, you can do it more than nine times, but that is a good starting place because nine is made up of three threes and considered to be a very auspicious number in Daoist practice. You will feel refreshed and renewed by this practice. You can do it any time your energy seems low or obstructed.

Remember to keep that sense of stillness and peacefulness that you felt in your stillness practice in your moving practice as well.

9

Standing Meditation

I WILL INTRODUCE a few of the basic standing practices here. There are some similarities between standing and sitting meditation practices, but the fact that we are standing up does make a difference. We will be moving a bit in these practices.

In both sitting and standing practice, we still connect with earth qi and heaven qi, especially through the yongquan pressure point at the balls of our feet and through the baihui pressure point at the top of our head. It does take a fair amount of energy to do the standing practices for any length of time, so it is best to begin with a few minutes and work up from there. I have seen practitioners do standing meditation for up to one or even two hours!

Basic Standing Practice

BEGIN BY STANDING with your feet shoulder-width apart, in a relaxed yet upright manner. Relax your whole body, from the top of your head (at the baihui point) to the "bubbling spring" (yongquan) pressure point on the balls of your feet, one body part at a time. Relax the top of your head down through your face, throat, upper chest, upper arms, belly and lower back, waist, upper thighs, lower legs, all the way down to your feet and even your toes. It may take a while to do this at first, but with time you will be able to relax more quickly. You can also shake out your arms and legs or bounce a few times on your heels to get all the energy in your body to loosen up and begin to flow more easily. (Another great way to begin the standing meditation practice is the grounding/rooting practice you learned in chapter 6.)

- Once you get a good, rooted feeling, you can pull up earth qi through the yongquan pressure points on the bottom of your feet, as if you were drawing up through a straw, up through your legs and thighs and waist, all the way into your lower dantian. Fill your lower dantian with the good healing energy of the living, breathing earth.
- Feel your entire body filling with this gentle yin energy. You can release any toxic or stressful energy you have in your body or psyche down through your feet and let it flow into the earth. You can also use the intention of your mind to open the baihui pressure point at the top of your head, allowing celestial qi from the sun, the moon, and the stars into your system.
- Draw or direct that celestial energy in through your baihui and let it flow gently into your body through

your chong mai, the central channel that runs through the very center of your body from the top of your head all the way down to your perineum (*hui yin*), where it connects with your lower dantian. Stand this way for a few moments, relaxing into the feeling of being fed by the earth and the stars.

- Then bring your arms out in front of you, palms facing in, as if you were holding a big ball of qi, or as if you were hugging a tree. One way to do this is to hold your arms up at shoulder level, elbows slightly bent, with your palms facing your heart center (*shen*). If this is too difficult, you can hold your arms at waist height with your palms facing your lower dantian.
- Tuck your pelvis in a little, as if you were sitting on a high stool, and bend your knees slightly. Imagine you are holding a large ball of qi between your palms, arms, and torso. You can even imagine that you are spinning the ball in a clockwise direction. You may find that you have an even stronger sense of the qi when you do this.

  This type of standing meditation is often called "standing like a post" (z*han zhuang*). Sometimes it is even called "hugging a tree," because it is as if you are putting your arms around a tree. Of course, you can actually hug a tree and gain extra benefit as you exchange qi with the tree.

Stand like this for five or ten minutes at first. You can gradually extend that to twenty or even thirty minutes or more. It is a good way to strengthen your kidney/adrenal energy, which will give you more day-to-day energy.

You can also add a bit of movement to your standing practice. Here is a standing practice that I learned on Wudang Mountain in China.

Wudang Mountain Standing Practice

- Stand facing forward as in the previous standing practice; then turn your waist and upper body slowly to the right while turning the large qi ball over, ending with your left palm over your right. Take nine deep breaths.
- Then turn slowly to the left while turning the large qi ball over, ending with your right palm over your left. Take nine deep breaths.
- Do this at least three times in each direction. You can, of course, do more than that. This is a great way to really connect with the qi in the large qi ball.
- Then turn to the front again and hold the ball out in front of you as before.
- To end the meditation, bring your palms together, resting on the abdomen, in front of your lower dantian and take at least nine deep breaths, sealing the qi that you have gathered into this important energy center.

Another way to do this practice is to stand with your back against a tree and lace your fingers together in front of your lower dantian. Feel yourself breathing with the tree. (Yes, trees do breathe in their own way.)

10

Walking Meditation

WE CAN TURN any activity into a meditation. All it takes is adjusting your focus, slowing down, and adopting a view of *wu wei* (actionless or effortless action). Wu wei, one of the most important principles in Daoism, is about not forcing, not overextending, not overdoing, but expending just enough energy and time to get done what needs to be done and not any more. In this way you will avoid exhausting yourself physically or even emotionally. Walking meditation is a great example.

Walking Meditation Practice

YOU CAN DO THIS walking practice on a sidewalk, but it is better if you can walk on a hiking trail or barefoot on the beach.

- Begin walking and pay special attention as you put one foot in front of the other. You may have to adjust your walking speed. Try not to go too fast. This is not speed-walking! Move slowly. But going too slowly can also be a problem. Find the pace that gives you a sense that you are moving along actively without tiring. Be conscious of your feet connecting to the living, breathing earth, even if you are walking on concrete.

Be conscious of your weight as it moves from one foot to another. Be aware that as you step and put your weight on the ball of your foot, you are also connecting to your yongquan pressure point, the first point on the kidney meridian. By putting pressure here, you are stimulating your kidney/adrenal organs, just as we did in the standing practice.

- Fold your thumbs into the center of your hand and close your fingers loosely around them. Keep your head up and drink in your surroundings. Be conscious of your weight shifting from side to side and of connecting to the earth with each step. While walking, be aware of where you are putting your feet, but at the same time don't forget to look up at your surroundings. Swing your arms naturally by your side, but not too vigorously. It is all a matter of balance. Indeed, this is a great way to describe the basic Daoist lifestyle.
- Look up at the sky. Notice whether it is full of clouds or birds or blue, blue sky. Look around you when you pass trees, or people, or even dogs. Pay attention to where you are going, where you have been, and exactly where you are at any given moment in time.

Take your time in this timeless time, if only for a little bit.

11

Water Meditation

HERE IS A MEDITATION that will allow you to feel a sense of the watercourse way, an important principle in Daoism. A crucial aspect of this meditation is that you move very slowly. Don't rush any of the steps. Keep the idea of *manzou* (going slowly) all the way through the practice. Complete this meditation either sitting or lying down.

Water Meditation Practice

IMAGINE YOURSELF lying on the earth beside a little stream. Relax, close your eyes, and listen to the water as it flows merrily along right next to you.

- Allow the sounds of the dancing water to fill your entire being. Feel a sense of how the water inside of you relates and perhaps even communicates with the water flowing by you. Let its watery qi speak to your own watery qi!

- Then, after a time, slowly and gently allow your body to simply roll over the bank of the stream and enter the current of the water. Feel it carry you along on its dancing way. Feel the coolness and softness of the water, while at the same time feeling it holding you up, supporting you, embracing you.
- Allow yourself to let go and let the water carry you along. Feel yourself become a water being, just like the fish and otters and other water beings that inhabit the water with you. Feel yourself flow along with the stream, flowing continuously downhill, down to the sea, to Source, to Dao.
- Feel your water being as you flow over the sand and the stones of the stream. Sometimes you may encounter an obstruction, like a beaver dam or a large rock. When this happens, relax and allow the water to slowly raise its levels until you can flow over the obstruction or around the rock, always joyfully moving along on your own playful, watery way.
- At some point, feel yourself entering a larger stream. Feel the pace of the water picking up as it flows along down to the nearest river, where you and the stream join with that larger body of water. Now you can sense a state of more strength and power in the water. Feel it carry you along, allowing your sense of self to become larger and stronger, while at the same time feeling that fresh and easy feeling of being supported and carried by the water. Feel the water in your own body blend with the water you are in. Feel the current picking up

a little more, though still gentle, still supportive.

- Now feel yourself as a river entering the Mother ocean, as if you were returning to Source, to Dao. Feel your water being expand greatly as you merge with the endless ocean, the eternal source of all life. Take some time to glory in the feeling of expansion and the warm embrace of the Mother ocean. Feel your small sense of self expand into a greater sense of self. Feel yourself become the ocean itself.
- After a time, feel the warmth of the sun shining down on you, drawing your water being up into the sky, where it joins with other water beings and becomes a cloud floating gently over the earth.
- Now feel your water body flow down to the earth in the form of rain, there to join once again with the brooks and streams and rivers and oceans of the world.

Take some time with this meditation, going at your own pace. Let yourself feel each step in a really sensuous way.

Of course if you find yourself by a stream or a river or an ocean, that's even better. But even if you are not physically by a body of water, you can always conjure one up in your mind; or else you can play a recording of the sound of water.

12

Organ Balancing Meditation

THE ORGAN BALANCING MEDITATION practice is unique to Daoism. Daoists see our organs as both energetic and physical forms. In some translations of traditional Chinese medicine texts, you will see the phrase *heavenly orbs* or *spheres* to describe the organs. Also, our emotions are seen as *energetic states*. The tools of traditional Chinese medicine—acupuncture, herbs, qigong, massage, meditation, internal alchemy, and diet—all use energetic healing to recover from physical, emotional, and even psychological problems.

This organ balancing meditation practice is part of the Wu Xing (Five Transformational Phases) school of Daoism, sometimes referred to as the Five Elements school; though as you will see, the word *element* refers to much more than merely elements.

In Daoist practice there is a long list of attributes associated with each organ—color, direction, element, season, flavor, power animal, and negative as well as positive emotional tones—to name just a few. We will be using some of these in the following meditation. At first it may take a little imagination to do this practice, but in time you will see and experience yourself and your various organs in just this energetic way. We will be covering the energetic properties of the five major *zhang* organs: the liver, heart, spleen, lungs, and kidneys. They are paired with five *fu* organs as well—the liver with gallbladder, the heart with the pericardium, the spleen with the pancreas, the lungs with the large intestine, and the kidneys with the bladder. By working on strengthening and clearing our zhang organs, we will energetically strengthen our other organs as well.

Organ Balancing Meditation Practice

TO BEGIN, lie down or sit quietly, breathing gently and slowly from your belly, eyes closed, seeing with the mind's eye.

- Imagine a cloud of light hovering just above your head at the baihui pressure point. Feel it floating there for a moment or two. Then let it slowly sink down through the top of your head and the right side of your body to just below your right rib cage to your liver. Here it becomes a rich green, the green of spring, of new growth, of expansion and free-flowingness.

  As you meditate, picture your liver as a rich green color, limber and flexible, and able to help you move through the challenges in your life. Picture yourself as the rich new growth of spring—resilient, strong, and supple. The energy of the liver is "moving forward."

The liver element is wood, the wood of plants, grasses, and trees. It is associated with the east, the direction of the sunrise. It is the season of spring, of new beginnings and of new adventures. The power animal associated with the liver is the green dragon. Its virtue is kindness or compassion.

The liver regulates the functions of our nervous system. Besides acting as a filter for the toxins in our system, it regulates movement within our body. The ability of blood, lymph, qi, and even emotions to move freely throughout our system is governed by our liver. The liver also governs our ability to move freely through our emotions and the challenges of our lives. It is also associated with the sense of sight. Imbalances in the liver can manifest in vision problems, diminished eyesight, or lack of perception. This can be a lack of insight or inner seeing, not just physical vision.

The negative emotion associated with the liver is anger. When our liver gets too tight and heated up by alcohol or other toxins, the heat rises into our head and produces anger and even rage.

It is very helpful to spend a few moments sending thoughts and feelings of gratitude to your liver, which is working for us 24/7 throughout our lives, especially if we do not degrade it through an unhealthy lifestyle. Some Daoists use the practice of an inner smile to send these feelings of gratitude. Remember, with gratitude comes grace. When our heart is open in gratitude, a feeling of calm and joy suffuses our being.

- Now the energy cloud moves up to the left side of your chest to your heart. Here it becomes a bright, vibrant red. Red is the season of summer when life is at its peak. It is a joyous, creative time when the bright sun shines mightily down on us all. Feel this season in your heart as the red cloud pulses slowly in your chest. The element is fire, the fire of controlled passion and creativity. Its direction is south. In traditional Chinese medicine the heart is thought of as the emperor of all the other organs.

- Picture this vibrant red cloud lightly lying on your heart, filling it with joy and purpose, openness and creativity. Sit and relax for a bit and allow yourself to feel this deep within you. In Daoist practice, it is said that "qi follows *yi*," that energy goes with the mind. Wherever you put your attention is where the energy will go. This is why it is important to keep our thoughts positive and supportive so that this will be the kind of energy we will attract and create within ourselves. Remember to spend a few moments sending thoughts and feelings of gratitude to your heart.

The heart's job is to keep the blood moving freely throughout our body. It is also the home of shen, or spirit. It is that which makes us human, that which gives us consciousness. The power animal of the heart is the red phoenix. The energy of the heart is moving upward. Its virtue is what we might call civilization: the ability to live alongside others in a mannerly way.

The negative aspect of an unbalanced heart energy can be expressed as too much talking, talking too fast, or even the inability to express oneself clearly. The negative emotion associated with the heart is hysteria, or joy taken to an extreme. The positive, which we are emphasizing right now, is joy, expansion, and creativity.

- Next, move the energy cloud down the left side of your abdomen to your spleen area. Here the cloud turns into a deep, earthy yellow. Take the time to allow yourself to feel your empathy and connection to the earth and to all living beings. Feel the groundedness of your being. Remember to spend a few moments sending thoughts and feelings of gratitude to your spleen.

The spleen element is earth; its time is the pause or transition between seasons. It is the grounding force in our being. The energy of the spleen is being still. The power animal of the spleen is the yellow dragon. Its virtue is honesty, faithfulness, and integrity.

The spleen rules our digestion, extracting the qi from what we eat and drink (*gu qi*). It also helps us digest our life experiences. The negative emotion associated with the spleen is worry or self-absorption. The positive emotion is empathy and our connection with all life, what the Daoists call *wan wu*, "the ten thousand beings."

- Now move the energy cloud up to your chest and into your lungs. When it reaches your lungs it turns a bright white. It hovers there, within your lungs, filling them with vital, healing energy.

- Picture your lungs becoming strong and healthy, expanding easily with each breath, sending out protective qi to all parts of your body, and each cell expanding and contracting as you breathe deeply and slowly. We picture and feel the attributes of courage and the ability to surrender as we see a bright white cloud of energy lying loosely upon our lungs. Remember to spend a few moments sending thoughts and feelings of gratitude to your lungs.

The season that corresponds to the lungs is autumn, the time when the natural world is preparing for the long sleep of winter. The corresponding direction is west; the element is metal or gold; and the power animal is the white tiger. Its virtue is uprightness and selflessness. The energy of the lungs is contracting or condensing.

Our lungs rule our respiration—our ability to extract oxygen, other nutrients, and additionally qi—from the air around us. They are also connected to our skin, the largest organ of our body; and they govern our *wei,* or protective qi, guarding us against flu and colds or infectious diseases, what the Chinese call "outside evils."

The negative emotion connected with the lungs is grief. It is here we feel our sadness, our loss. And while we acknowledge the importance of connecting to that grief and not denying or suppressing it, at this time we would like to emphasize the positive emotions of courage and the ability to surrender deeply to each moment.

- Next, move to your lower back, to the kidneys (also associated with the adrenals). Here the energy cloud turns a deep blue-black. Sit for a few moments and allow yourself to breathe deeply into your kidneys. With each breath, fill them with powerful qi so they will be able to hold you up, both in your daily life and in all your endeavors.

The kidney element is water, and the direction is north. The season is winter (the time when earth energy is dormant and deep), and the power animal is the black turtle. Its virtue is wisdom.

The kidneys are said to open to the ears, and an imbalance here can manifest as hearing problems or being unable to understand what others are saying to you. The kidneys are a strong part of our root system; their energy is returning to the root. The negative emotions associated with the kidneys are fear and anxiety. But in this practice we will emphasize the ability of the kidney energy to instill willpower and the ability to deal with our lives in a positive and creative fashion.

The kidney/adrenal area is the seat of our will. It is also the source of our day-to-day energy, the pilot light beneath our furnace. Here we store our sense of will and determination, our backbone. Our kidneys are also where we store our prenatal qi, or *jing,* which is very important to our physical and mental development. In addition, it is the repository of our generative or sexual energy. Because the very pulse of life starts here, it is important that we work on creating strong kidney energy and not dissipate it through a self-abusive lifestyle.

Remember to spend a few moments sending thoughts and feelings of gratitude to your kidneys/adrenals.

- From here you can go back to the liver and cycle through the organs again or let the energy cloud ascend back up through your baihui.

In this meditation we have paid deep attention to the organ systems that work so well for us, moment to moment. We have thanked them for their wonderful work, and we have imbibed their valuable qualities of flexibility, free flow, joy, creativity, empathy, groundedness, courage, surrender, and the willpower to face the challenges of our life experiences positively and creatively.

Another way you can do this meditation is to go through the bulleted practice sequences again and as you cycle through each one, ask:

The liver: What is holding me back from being flexible and adaptable?
The heart: What is getting in the way of my joy and creativity?
The spleen: How can I experience myself as being more rooted and grounded in my life?
The lungs: How can I connect with the courage to move forward in my life and leave my grief behind?
The kidneys: How can I let go of my fears and experience myself as having more backbone?

Really spend some time with each question. Ask it, then give yourself time to receive an answer or guidance from your higher Dao self. There is no need to rush through this process. You have all the time in the world to explore this area of your psyche. Also, if you find that there is a certain organ or emotional state that you are weak in, which often happens, you can spend a little more time in that one.

Do this practice daily or whenever you feel a need to get in touch with those qualities that the organs represent. In time you will become sensitized to the health, vitality, and inner integrity not only of your inner organs but of your emotions as well.

13

Six Healing Sounds

ONE WAY THAT WE CAN strengthen our organs is by doing the six healing sounds, an ancient shamanic energy practice that uses sounds or vibrations to enhance, invigorate, and heal each organ system. These sounds balance, detoxify, and strengthen each of our major organs, which can also bring our emotions into balance.

These sounds can be made aloud or even subvocally. The vibration is the most important part. Some people find that making the sounds inaudibly is the most powerful way to utilize them. Chant each sound nine to thirty-six times or more, slowly and deeply. You can close your eyes and imagine each sound traveling to its main organ. If it helps, you can put your hands over each organ as you do so.

Six Healing Sounds Practice

- The healing sound of the liver is *xu* (pronounced "shoe") and is made by pursing the lips together and making the sound *shuuuuuu*. This sound calms and heals the qi of the liver and stabilizes your emotions, especially anger.

- The healing sound of the heart is *ho* (pronounced "hoe"). Use it to supplement the heart qi and help quell the fire of the heart, induce calm, and stabilize your emotions. *Ho* can also give you a feeling of joy and lightness, as if you are quietly laughing.
- The healing sound of the spleen is *hu* (pronounced "who"). It can address digestive issues and help you to feel emotionally and energetically grounded.
- The healing sound of the lungs is *si* (pronounced "ssss," like a hissing snake). It clears and balances the qi of the lungs. This sound can also help ease grief and sadness.
- The healing sound of the kidneys is *chu* (pronounced "chew"). Make a *chu* sound to assuage fear and panic and to revitalize your kidneys/adrenals for better day-to-day energy.
- The final healing sound is *xi* (pronounced "she"). This sound can help regulate the triple warmer, or *san jio.* The upper warmer is associated with our heart and lungs. The middle warmer relates to the middle of our body: our stomach, spleen, and liver. The lower warmer relates to the lower part of our body: our kidneys, bladder, and urogenital functions. The triple warmer is essential in transporting fluids throughout our body. It also helps balance and regulate our endocrine system.

By practicing these six sounds in a meditative and grounded fashion, we can affect change in our organ systems that will benefit us in a physical, emotional, psychological, and even spiritual way.

14

Tiger–Dragon Breathing Meditation

HERE'S A BREATHING MEDITATION that uses the powerful images and energetics of the tiger and the dragon. It is a way to connect with the solid qi of the earth and the graceful qi of the heavens. We really need both in our practice to be balanced and grounded. In this way, we experience ourselves—physically, emotionally, and energetically—in true yin/yang harmony: yin being the energy of the earth, of water, of darkness and inward direction; and yang being the energy of the sun, of fire and brightness, and of outward direction. We need both to function at a very high level in our lives. This simple breathing qigong practice is one way to do just that.

Before you begin the meditation, think to yourself: *Do I need more yang to balance my nature, or do I need more yin?* Whatever you decide (and it can change from time to time or from day to day), spend some time just inhaling tiger and exhaling tiger or inhaling dragon and exhaling dragon.

Tiger–Dragon Breathing Meditation Practice

SIT, STAND, OR LIE DOWN, paying close attention to the incoming and outgoing movement of your breath. Keep your breathing as slow and deep as you can while still breathing comfortably.

- As you inhale, breathe in the energy of the tiger as the root of the earth. Think of the solidity and strength of the tiger. Remember, in the five transformation phases system, the tiger represents the direction of the west, the element gold, the color white, and the lungs—our main organs of respiration. It also represents the quality of courage.
- Then, when you exhale, breathe out the energy of the dragon as the root of heaven, as well as the openness and fluidity of the dragon. See the dragon as a green dragon that represents the direction of the east, of sunrise, of new directions and possibilities, and of the element wood.
- Now just put your attention on your inhales and exhales. Inhale: Think of the strength and solidity of the tiger. Exhale: Think of the openness and fluidity of the dragon. Then say to yourself "tiger" on inhale and "dragon" on exhale. Spend some time just breathing in the image and energy of the tiger and dragon.

After doing it this way for a time, you can change the inhalation to dragon and the exhalation to tiger. Take the time to really see yourself as that tiger or dragon. Yes, tigers can be fierce, but here we are connecting to the righteous fierceness of being a force for good in the world. In Asia dragons are seen as auspicious, not dangerous. Here we can connect with a beautiful, graceful, dancing way to live our lives. As you do the practice, see yourself as both tiger and dragon, exemplifying the strengths of each one. Picture yourself as a fierce, strong tiger as well as a fluid, beautiful dragon.

You can also use the mantra XIN PING, QI HE, pronounced "shin, ping, chee, he (as in 'huh')," that means "heart peaceful or calm, qi harmonious or balanced." Say the first part to yourself as you inhale and the second part as you exhale.

Spend as much time as you can with this meditation, at least ten to twenty minutes.

15

Planetary Expansion Meditation

THIS IS AN EXERCISE in what is called in Daoist practice "the qi follows the yi," or "energy follows the mind." Our qi or vital energy can move in all sorts of ways. It can expand and contract, following the direction of our mind, which is why it is so important to keep a positive mindset as much as possible.

So often we experience ourselves as just our physical body, maybe with a little of our thoughts as well. Laozi tells us that we would have fewer problems if we did not have such a limited sense of self. In other words, who and what we are encompasses so much more than just our physical body and thought processes. This meditation and qigong practice gives us an experience of expanding what we usually identify as our self into a much greater dimension.

Planetary Expansion Meditation

SETTLE YOUR BREATH and focus on your lower dantian. Feel your abdomen expand and then contract with each breath.

- Going very slowly, begin to use each inhale to expand your sense of self until it fills the entire room you are in. Slowly expand your sense of self even more until it grows to the size of the building you are in. Really take the time to energetically experience yourself as becoming a larger and larger being.
- After a while, expand your sense of self further until it is the size of the entire town you are in. Then expand it even more until it is the size of the hemisphere you are in.
- After a while, expand it once again until it is the size of the entire planet.

  What does it feel like to be a planet? Do your worries seem to become smaller and smaller as you become vaster and vaster? Does this new perspective give you deeper insights into your life? Does it free up some reservoirs of qi?

  What does it feel like to be a planet giving life to all sorts of life forms that depend on you? How does it feel to relate to other planets that are gently turning in space all around you? Does it perhaps help put some of your problems and concerns in a different light?

Does it make you feel more powerful, stronger, able to let go of your problems and concerns? Does it give you new perspectives into your life and being?

- Then expand your sense of self again until it reaches far out to space, taking in all the planets in our solar system.
- Then once more, expand it until your sense of self encompasses the entire galaxy. Last, expand it until it fills the whole universe and all that it contains.

  Really feel your sense of self expand far beyond your body and what you have always thought of as your self. Feel it mentally and energetically as your sense of self grows to contain all of life. Go slowly and try to really feel this expansion of yourself in a very real and tactile way. Try to stay in this state for a little while. Enjoy the feeling of being immense, of containing multitudes, of being so large that small problems remain small problems. Feel the wonderful perspective of being so large and so complete in a way that you may have never felt before.
- To end the meditation, begin drawing in your energy on each inhalation. Bring your sense of self in slowly, from the universe to the galaxy, to the planet, to the hemisphere, to the town, to the building, to the room, to your own body.

This practice offers you a sense of expansiveness of spirit as well as qi body. It may seem strange at first, imagining yourself as containing the universe, but there is a seed of Dao within you that is just that.

16

Flying Meditation

I RECEIVED THIS MEDITATION IN A DREAM, so it does not come from a traditional source like the others, but I thought I would share it here for fun! The goal of this practice is to introduce a feeling of lightness and buoyancy. As in the planetary expansion meditation, it is a way for us to experience our energy body, which extends beyond the confines of our physical body. It is a way of inducing a light heart, a lightness of being, which we can then extend into the rest of our life.

Flying Meditation Practice

- Begin your meditation as you normally do, but this time when you inhale allow your lower dantian to fill up like a balloon. Then feel your energy body lift off the cushion (known as a "cloud chair" in Daoism) or chair you are sitting on at least a few inches.
- Then, when you exhale, drop your energy body gently down to the cushion or chair again. (In my dream I was actually lifting off the ground with each inhale.)

In qigong we have a saying: "Imagination becomes reality." This means that by using our imagination (as in imagining healing light entering the body and exiting as black smoke, as described in the healing light meditation), over time these things actually begin happening. Many ancient Daoist sages are said to have been able to fly off on the back of a dragon or ride upon the wind.

- End this meditation as before: Briskly rub your palms together thirty-six times before rubbing your hands up and down your face to bring yourself out of the meditation mode. Then allow yourself to rise from your cushion or chair with a lightness of being and a feeling of uplifted energy.

17

Empty Vessel Meditation

IN THIS MEDITATION PRACTICE we allow ourselves to become empty vessels. Laozi describes Dao like this:

> *Dao is an empty vessel;*
> *it is used but never exhausted.*
> *It is the fathomless source*
> *of the ten thousand beings!*[16]

In another chapter Laozi tells us it is the empty space inside the cup or bowl that makes it useful. Sometimes we need to empty ourselves of all our important issues, thoughts, and ideas and allow ourselves to become empty so that we may be open to receiving something of value and genuine importance.

Empty Vessel Meditation Practice

YOU CAN DO THIS meditation sitting or lying down. If lying down, be careful you don't fall asleep. Sleeping and meditation are two different things!

Prepare for the meditation. Begin by following your breath and focusing on your lower dantian until you feel grounded and settled. Then stop focusing anywhere.

- Allow your focus to soften and expand. Then just sit with no expectations, no agenda, and no fear. Calmly abide in stillness, empty and ready to receive. You may find that you are given information or guidance from your higher or Dao self at this time. It may come as a feeling or perhaps as a solution to a problem you have been dealing with. It does not come from your everyday mind but something much higher, or perhaps as a different form of intelligence than your day-to-day mind.
- If you cannot remember it and need to write it down, do so quickly without pausing to think about it, then go back to the meditation. Once you feel you have come to the end of the session, end the meditation in the same way as before: Briskly rub your palms together thirty-six times before rubbing your hands up and down your face.

You may be surprised at what you will receive in this practice. It may come in words, it may come as a feeling, as simply knowing, as an inspiration, or you may just have a feeling of being filled with something beyond words or description. Either way is a gift from Dao to you.

Zhuangzi says,

Dwell in the empty chamber within, which is full of light. By dwelling in this stillness, great blessings will come your way. If you do not rest there, your mind will keep racing madly like a wild horse. But if you keep yourself centered and still, deep within this place, and allow your thinking mind to dwell outside, you will attract helpful spirits, and divine beings will come to your aid![17]

18

Holy Flowers Meditation

THIS MEDITATION uses the visualization of a sacred grove filled with many hundreds of flowers. These flowers represent spiritual growth. It is when we allow the colors and qi of all the blooming flowers to flow into our body and being that we can receive an experience of healing.

Holy Flowers Meditation Practice

IMAGINE YOURSELF sitting in the middle of a sacred forest, surrounded by hundreds and hundreds of flowers not yet in bloom. As you sit on the good green earth, feel yourself being supported by the lush, thick grass, like a soft and living carpet. The sky above you is a deep, deep blue.

- Look around you at the hundreds and hundreds of flower buds that surround you, in every color you can imagine: reds, yellows, greens, purples, blues, white, even black, silver, and gold.

A warm and gentle breeze blows past you as you sit and wait for the flowers to open and blossom. But for now, you just sit on the soft, green, living earth and breathe deeply, slowly, and gently. Relax your whole body and being, from the very top of your head (at the baihui pressure point) to the very bottom of your feet (at the yongquan pressure point). Take your time to really feel yourself relaxing while also holding yourself up. Relaxing does not mean collapsing.

- Sitting and breathing the warm air and breeze, feel yourself supported by the good green earth as the flowers suddenly start to bloom all around you. As the flowers bloom, feel yourself begin to bloom along with them. Feel your own internal power (qi) bloom and get stronger as the flowers around you open themselves completely to the warm, life-giving sun. Just sit and breathe in all the scents of these flowers.
- Begin to collect all the colors and scents and qi of the flowers straight into your lower dantian, letting them fill you with their powerful qi. Feel the colors, the scents, and the powerful qi of all the flowers begin to condense themselves in your lower dantian, filling it with earth and sky qi.

Now just sit and enjoy the feeling of the earth below you, the warm sky above you, and the flowers as they bloom all around you and within you.

- To end the meditation, place your palms over your dantian and slowly move them in a circular motion, nine times one direction and nine times in the other, sealing all that good qi and flower medicine in your body and being.

19

Tea (Cha Dao) Meditation

> Tea opens the heart, clears the mind, settles the soul, and illuminates the spirit.[18]
>
> —WU DE

THE TEA CEREMONY has been a big part of both Zen and Daoism for thousands of years. There is even a saying in Zen that "you cannot know the taste of Zen without knowing the taste of tea."

To practice *cha dao,* or the way of tea, you don't need special equipment or even special teas. You just need a teakettle, a wastewater bowl, a cup, and whatever tea you enjoy drinking. For those who already practice cha dao, *pu'er*—an aged, fermented tea from China that has numerous health benefits—is usually the tea of choice, but you can use any tea that you enjoy. What is most important is the spirit you bring to the ceremony, not what tea you use or even the ceremonial actions themselves.

To quote my tea-master friend, Paul (Po) Rosenberg,

> You should be able to take a tin can and put a Lipton tea bag in it and serve it to someone you care about, across

the table, with absolute presence, love, and a sense of deep quiet, and it can be a magical experience. You can also drink one-hundred-year-old rare tea with someone who is not working from that deep place in them and it's not very fun. I would rather drink from the tin can any day and be with someone who is in touch both with their humanity and their divinity.[19]

In the Daoist tradition we practice, we call the tea ceremony *pin ming lun dao,* meaning "savor tea, discuss Dao." The first character, *pin,* means "savor" and is made up of three squares, or three mouths. The tea ceremony is not just drinking tea (*he cha*) but really taking the time to *savor* the tea, letting it become a part of our body and spirit. To quote one of my tea teachers, Zhongxian Wu, "Pin is also the way of study and meditation in classical Chinese culture. This is a way of classical Chinese spiritual cultivation, called Cha Dao (the Dao of Tea)—a way of reaching enlightenment through drinking tea."[20] The second character, *ming,* means "good quality tea" and is also an ancient word for tea. The final two characters, *lun dao,* mean "discuss Dao," or share from deep within your own heart. This can be sharing poems, stories, or whatever is coming up for you in that moment.

Daoism is about connecting with nature—the great nature without and our own beautiful spiritual nature within. In the great tradition of Dao we have many tools to help us enter the state of what the ancient sages called "entering Dao" or "returning to Source." Practices such as qigong, taiji, calligraphy, music, dance, and certainly the tea ceremony are all powerful tools to not only approach but also connect deeply with the divine Source, or Dao. In the following *gongfu* tea ceremony (*gongfu cha*) you will be able to connect with not only the spirit of tea but with the Dao itself.

We often use very small teapots and very small cups as well. Ideally, these would be made of Yixing clay that has been used in China for hundreds of years for brewing tea. It is very porous and retains heat quite well. As a matter of fact, it is said that after using a Yixing pot for many years it will be filled with the oils and fragrance of the tea, and we could just pour hot water into the teapot and pour out tea! But it is not necessary to have Yixing pottery to get a lot out of your tea practice. You can use any pot or cups you have on hand. Remember, it's the spirit you bring to it that makes the tea ceremony special.

Pin Ming Lun Dao Tea Ceremony

AS THE WATER in your teakettle slowly begins heating up, you can honor the work of Dr. Emoto, a Japanese scientist who did many experiments with sending different types of energy and intention into water. He had his students send both positive and negative energy into water. Then he froze the water and looked at it under a microscope. He found that positive energy created beautiful crystalline forms. Negative energy, on the other hand, created really gnarly, lopsided forms. So it is a good idea to send good thoughts and good qi into your tea water, which will give the tea better qi.

These instructions are for pu'er tea that requires we discard the first steeping, but you can use any kind of tea you like and skip the steeping rinses.

- Fill your teakettle with water and put it on to heat. When the water is hot, fill your teapot with water to warm it up. Let the water heat up the pot for a moment or two, then pour it out into a bowl or other receptacle.
- Fill the teapot with pu'er tea and let the water and the tea leaves get to know each other for a moment. Pour this first steeping out into the wastewater container or, if you are outside, as an offering to the earth—the earth who gave of herself for the tree and the leaves to grow—so that you may spend some time in communion with this wonderful brew.

  The first steeping rinses the leaves of any dust or impurities. It also washes out some of the caffeine (if that is an issue with you). Also, if your tea is a compressed brick, as is a lot of pu'er, the hot water helps the leaves to soften and "wake up."
- Now pour some more water into the teapot and let it dance with the leaves for a moment or so, then pour some of the magical elixir into your cup. Hold your cup with your thumb and first finger, with the ring finger supporting it, in front of your heart center. This way you can connect the qi of the tea (*cha qi*) with your own heart center. It is also a way to give thanks to the earth that grew the trees or plants, the sky that

shone down on them, the rain that fed them so well, the people who gathered and processed the leaves, and the pathway from that place in China or wherever the tea came from to your own cup right there in your hand, remembering that with gratitude comes grace.

- Next, look at the tea, noticing its color. By connecting your eyes with the tea, you will create a deeper connection to your heart center. This heart center is our spiritual center as well as the place of cognitive thought and of memories and dreams. It gives our lives meaning and links us with our divine Source. The heart center resides in our heart and can be seen through our eyes, the windows of the soul.
- Then smell the tea, allowing the fragrance of the tea to cross your blood-brain barrier and connect with your qi body. Qi itself is the life force that fills every living being. It is what animates us, what gives us life. It warms us and directs all our movements.
- Lastly, taste the tea, connecting the tea qi with your earth body, or *jing*. Our jing is our prenatal qi that we receive from our parents at conception. It is our constitutional energy as well as our sexual energy. It regulates our hormonal and reproductive system, controls our growth throughout our lives, and regulates our central nervous system.

When you first taste the tea, do so with three small sips: the first with the tip of your tongue, the second with the middle of your tongue, and the last with the back of your tongue. You may be amazed at all the different flavors you will discover this way. Drink the tea slowly and with full presence. If you are sharing tea with others, take a few moments to drink the tea in silence before you start speaking.

Take all the time you need to be fully present with the tea and your guests or just your own simple self, allowing yourself to move out of time and into the timeless time. In this way the art of preparing and drinking tea becomes a full meditation and even a spiritual practice!

HERE IS A POEM I wrote some years ago about a tea session as a celebration.

Every Tea Should Be a Time of Celebration

When we drink tea (pin ming)
we celebrate
the magical transformation
of leaf and water
contained in the cup or bowl
from which we drink.
The tea leaves that appear
so dead and dry
have, when paired with hot water,
become transformed

from dry dead leaf
to a living liquor,
connecting the drinker
with the land
that the tree or bush
grew from,
the hands that picked
bud and leaves,
who then processed it,
itself a hard labor.
Then the seller of the tea,
then to us,
our own hands and mouth
touching the tea,
our own spirits becoming
calm and centered
as we drink the magical brew.
So it is that we celebrate
this coming together
of hand and heart,
of land and leaf,
of sunlight and moonlight
and our own sweet selves.
We give thanks and praises
for the opportunity
and blessings
to share ourselves
with the ancient magic
of water, earth,

and sunlight, so bright,
so life-giving.
We celebrate
the coming together
of all these things,
these gifts given freely
of the earth and the sky.
In this way every tea
becomes a celebration
of gratitude and grace.

20

Great Mother Meditation

THIS MEDITATION can help connect us to what Laozi, in describing Dao, calls the Great or Primal Mother. In chapter 20 of the *Daodejing,* Laozi explains why the sage is different from all the other people running around in the rat race who look at him like he is thickheaded and stupid. He is different, he says, because he is "nourished by the Great Mother."

The image of the universe as a Great Mother is found in many religious cultures—Mother Mary, the bodhisattvas Guanyin and Green Tara, etc. The image of the universe not as a cold collection of gaseous forms but as a loving mother has comforted humans throughout history. This is what makes this practice so powerful.

Here are two different meditations to connect to the Great or Primal Mother. Each is a bit different from the other and will allow you to experience this powerful Mother energy in a different way.

Great Mother Meditation, Part One

SIT OR LIE DOWN and begin your deep, slow dantian breathing.

- Feel your navel as being connected to the Great Mother of us all in a very real and energetic way. Feel an energetic umbilical cord connecting you with the great source of all life, the Great Mother. Allow yourself to begin feeling a flow of energy between you and the Great Mother. Draw deep sustenance from this connection.
- As you experience this state of being an infant in the womb of the Great Mother, feel how well you are fed by her. Draw on her strength and fill yourself with her power. Know that you are always connected to her through this energetic umbilical cord. Know that as a child of the Great Mother you are always and forever supported and loved.

  Your Great Mother is always there for you, sending you nothing but love and support. Feel how her wisdom guides and protects you. Relax and feel yourself floating gently in the womb of the Great Mother, feeling safe and loved with no judgment. Spend some time here in the womb of the Great Mother allowing yourself to relax and enjoy her warm embrace.

You can always remind yourself to reconnect to the Great Mother at any time. She is always there for you.

Great Mother Meditation, Part Two

SIT OR LIE DOWN quietly, breathing deeply and slowly.

- Feel yourself become filled with qi and spirit, as though you were pregnant with child. Envision yourself as a mother giving birth to a new version of yourself. (We all have an aspect of the Great or Primal Mother within us, even if we are male.) Welcome this new version of yourself with love.
- Feel yourself as a mother giving birth, constantly and eternally. This is your Dao self, and it is as real as anything you can see in the world around you, if not more so. Allow yourself the time to really experience yourself as this Primal Mother giving life and love to those around you as well as to yourself.
- Feed this new, infantile version of you with your good intentions and your wish to become a strong, clarified, balanced person—spiritually, emotionally, and physically. Ask yourself:
    - What old, stale parts of you do you need to let go of in order to be born anew?
    - What old patterns can you let go of so your true self can shine through?
    - How can you connect in a deep and real way to the Primal Mother of us all?

In *neidan,* or internal alchemy practice, we see the term *red baby* or *golden embryo* (*shengtai*). This is what is created at the highest stage of cultivation practice. It is birthing a new self. Just like a pregnant mother, we need to nourish ourselves with good spiritual nutrition. We need to be careful about what goes into our energetic body and what comes out. We need to protect ourselves from toxic energy, and we need to get the right amount of movement and stillness.

- When you feel you are finished, close the meditation as usual, rubbing your palms together thirty-six times and then rubbing them over your face. It is extremely important that you do not cut off these meditative and energetic states once you get up off your cushion. Keep them going throughout your day and throughout your life. Try to bring some of this experience of the Primal Mother into the rest of your life.

21

Seasonal Cultivation Practice

THIS IS ANOTHER PRACTICE from the Wuxing or Five Transformational Phases school of Daoism. In this system, as we saw in the Organ–Balancing Meditation, each season is associated with an element, organ, color, etc. In this chapter we will be focusing on some simple practices that can help us energetically align ourselves with each season.

Wood (Spring) Practice

WE BEGIN with the season of spring, the time of year when the new growth of trees, plants, flowers, and people begins to reach out toward the life-giving sun.

Face east as you do this practice in the morning. Sit, stand, or lie upon the earth in an area that has trees, bushes, flowers, or grass. If you cannot be outside, you can do this practice indoors, especially if you have a plant in your house or at least can look out of your window and see some grass or trees.

- Open your eyes wide and let the good, deep green color fill your vision. Allow the green color to fill your being with the energy of new growth.
- Feel your ability to flow freely through your day-to-day life and the challenges of your life. Allow your inner being to soften and become as flexible as a newly sprouted blade of grass.

Laozi tells us that when a plant is young it is very supple and bendable. Grass, when walked on, pops back up again. But as the plant ages, it becomes dry and brittle and breaks easily. So too do we. If we don't remain flexible in our body, it too will dry up and become brittle and we can easily break. Of course it is also extremely important, if not more so, that we don't become stuck and brittle in our mind.

Keeping our mind and heart open and flexible—open to new experiences, new ways of looking at the world, and new wisdom—will allow us to age as sages and not break like an old plant. Feel the excitement of the new sunrise, the new day, and the new opportunities each day brings.

Liver Detox Qigong

AS MENTIONED, the liver is associated with the season of spring—often a time when we need to slough off the energetic crud we have taken on during the winter season. Here is a special qigong practice you can do to strengthen and detoxify your liver.

- Stand with your knees as wide apart as your shoulders. Relax your whole body, from the top of your head (the baihui pressure point) to the bottom of your feet (the yongquan pressure point).
- From your lower dantian, guide qi down across your perineum and up your back (*du mai*) to the large bone at the top of your spine (*da zhui*).
- Split the qi into two streams and send it down across your shoulders, down your arms, and into your palms (*laogong*).
- Shift your weight to your left foot and step your right foot out toward a tree or plant or even some wooden furniture, placing your toes up against the tree. Of course it is best to do this practice with a living tree; but if there are no trees around and you do not have any plants in your home, you can use furniture, as it still has the element of wood in it.
- Gather qi by turning your palms up and raising your arms in front of you all the way up to the top of your head.
- Lower your palms over your baihui pressure point at the top of your head and beam healing qi into it.
- Open your shoulders and arms and, with your fingers facing each other and your palms facing down, slowly lower your arms down to your chest, guiding healing qi through your central channel (*chong mai*) as you do so.

- When your hands reach your chest level, pivot your waist so that your palms move over to your right side, and begin moving your palms down the right side of your body and down along the inside of your right leg. This is the path of the liver meridian. Feel any stress, toxic energy, or difficult feelings (especially if you have anger issues) flow right out of your big toe and into the tree (which will not harm the tree). In qigong this is called "dredging the channel" of your liver.
- To end the practice, return to a standing position and allow your arms to move down to your sides.

Do this exercise at least nine times, though you may need to do it more than that if you have a serious problem with your liver. You can do this exercise whenever you feel stuck or experience any sort of stressful, toxic energy in your body—especially in your liver.

Fire (Summer) Practice

IN THIS PRACTICE, you can face south or just stand or sit in the direction of the sun. Remember, if it is a cloudy day, the sun is still shining above the clouds! Stand facing the warm light of the sun, eyes closed lightly.

- Feel the gentle warmth of the sun grow inside you, filling you up with a feeling of joy and expansiveness.

You can also imagine "swallowing" the yang fire of the sun down into your dantian, though not more than nine times (so that you do not overload your system with fiery yang energy). To do this, move your head forward and "swallow" the sun energy with a gulping sound, and let it flow down to your lower dantian.

- Feel the energy of the sun, the supporter of all life on our beloved planet, as it shines down upon you and within you, filling you up with light and joy.

Here is another special meditation for healing or creating a peaceful heart. You can face the sun, but it can be done facing any direction.

- Sit quietly and breathe deeply, slowly, and softly.
- On each inhale say to yourself, either out loud or quietly, *xin ping* (heart peaceful), and on the exhale, say *qi he* (qi harmonious). If saying the Chinese is too difficult, just say the English phrases.
- Allow yourself to feel your spirit and mind expanding into a deep sense of joyful creativity.

Earth (The Time Between Each Season) Practice

STAND, SIT, or, even better, lie down on the good rich earth. Feel it holding you up and lovingly supporting you.

- Move your hands along the ground, your fingers caressing the earth. Feel how, when we lie upon the earth, we are connected to everyone else on our planet, as they also live their lives on it. Allow yourself to feel your deep connection to the living, breathing earth and to all the beings that live on it: the two-legged beings, the four-legged beings, the flying beings, the swimming beings, and the standing beings.
- Feel your groundedness and rootedness in the earth, or if you don't feel grounded, practice sending energetic roots from the bottom of your feet (yongquan) or the bottom of your spine down into the earth, at least three times the length of your body, as in the grounding/rooting practice in chapter 6.

Gold (Autumn) Practice

AUTUMN IS THE TIME to celebrate the harvest and enjoy the fruits of our hard work—not only the physical fruits but also the spiritual fruits that our efforts have sowed, cared for, and watched grow. This is a time to celebrate our bountiful harvest and enjoy the benefits of our hard work. Summer's expansion is winding down, and we can begin to draw our energy in a little so that we have a solid foundation for the winter season.

Our lungs are also connected to our *wei qi,* our protective qi, so now is a good time to pay attention to our health, especially for those of us who are prone to lung problems like bronchitis and asthma. Qigong breathing is extremely important now. Make sure you spend time on your breath practice and that it flows out into the rest of your life, especially at this time of year.

Autumn can be a very poignant time when the leaves turn colors, the air is crisp, and the smell of wood smoke fills the air. It is a good moment to look back on the rest of the year and feel good about what we have accomplished, both physically and spiritually. We can celebrate with friends and family and give thanks for all the wonderful gifts that our beloved planet Earth has given us!

Stand, sit, or lie down, paying close attention to your breath.

- Breathe deeply, allowing your lungs to fill all the way up, your abdomen expanding as you inhale and contracting as you exhale. This natural breathing is called *fantong huxi*, or "back to childhood breathing." Hold the breath for a few seconds, then breathe out, emptying your lungs completely. Pause for a few seconds before you take another breath. Imagine your lungs as the precious substance that they are. See them as shining gold. (Usually the element [*jin*] is translated as "metal," but it can also be translated as "gold." In the alchemical tradition gold is seen as a much warmer and more precious chemical element.) If you are counting breaths, remember that each inhale and exhale counts as one breath.

- Imagine you are breathing into your whole body, not just your abdomen and lungs or chest. Fill yourself up completely and empty yourself just as completely. Remember, it is not just oxygen you're breathing in but qi as well. Feel your qi stabilize and strengthen with each breath.

Water (Winter) Practice

UNLESS WE LIVE in a southern climate, winter is a cold time of year, so it is important to keep ourselves warm by paying attention to what we wear outside. If you are in a cold climate, be sure to wear a scarf to keep your neck warm. This can help protect you from "evil winds" or colds. Warm foods such as hot soup and cooked vegetables are also important.

Winter, the season of quiet contemplation, is an excellent time to strengthen our meditation practice. By being still, quiet, and closing down the outside influences in our lives, we can open doors to vast inner worlds. It is in this serene and tranquil mindset that we can discover the Dao, our source as well as our destination. In many traditional societies winter is the time to stay close to the fire, sharing food and stories with families and friends.

Here is a simple exercise for the kidneys/adrenals.

- First warm up your palms (*laogong*) by rubbing them briskly together thirty-six times. Then place them on your lower back, on each side of your backbone. Breathe the warmth of your palms deeply into your kidney/adrenal area. Then rub your palms over your lower back thirty-six times, circling up the inside and down the outside. This will help warm up your kidney/adrenal area.

- Sit, stand, or lie down and breathe slowly, deeply, and gently into your lower back. Don't try to make something happen. Follow the teaching of wu wei, or nonforce. On each inhale, imagine you are breathing directly into your kidney/adrenal area.

  By balancing and harmonizing your heart center as well as your qi system, you will feel much more at ease, and your kidney/adrenal energy will become stronger and less stressed. In general, take it easy and try not to stress your qi system or your emotional and psychological systems. Too much movement will exhaust one's qi, but excessive sitting will cause stagnation in the body. The key here is to not abandon one for the other, to experiment and see what the proper balance is for your own cultivation.

Think of this time as being in a warm and snug cocoon, just biding your time until spring comes and you are able to break out and open your beautiful wings to fly in the sun.

22

Turning the Light Around Meditation

THIS PRACTICE COMES FROM an ancient Daoist text called the *Secret of the Golden Flower* (*Taiyi Jinhua Zhongxi*), which uses the image of the golden flower of true awakening. Here we are taught how to close off our outer sight that is the primary way we interact and receive information from the world around us and instead rely on our inner sight.

The practice turns our attention/intention inward so we can experience what in Daoism is called "the original mind" or "the mind within the mind." The knowledge and experience we thereby receive is called "illumination" or "lit from within." By relying only on our outer sight, we often get deeply entangled with the world of duality, or what some call illusion.

Turning the Light Around Meditation

SIT ON A CUSHION OR A CHAIR. You can also do this practice standing up or even lying down.

- Place your tongue on the roof of your mouth and begin breathing deeply, slowly, and gently into your lower dantian.
- Close your eyes; in Daoist practice this is called "letting down the shades." Allow the wild horse of your mind to slow down until you are able to keep one thought in your mind. In Daoist practice this is described as "substituting ten thousand thoughts with one thought." A simple way to do this is to put your focus on your breath. Count each inhalation and each exhalation as one breath. You can count up to ten breaths or even thirty-six, but any more will be hard to focus on. Allow your breath to become so deep and natural that it feels as though you are being breathed.
- Now turn the light of your focus on your inner self; in Daoist texts this is called "internal shining," or *nei zhao*. When we turn our focus from the outside world, with all its entanglements, to our inner world, we may receive guidance and information from our higher or deeper self or even guiding spirits.

  Many people close their eyes when they want to deeply concentrate on something. Letting go of one of our senses can strengthen another one. (This is why many people who are blind have more acute hearing.) Allow this inner gaze to put you in touch with your original spirit.

- Keep deepening your gaze inward in a relaxed and open manner and gently explore what worlds may lie within you. See what experiences or inspiration may light themselves up in this way. You may get an image or a feeling or see actual lights when you do this practice. You may even get information or inspiration.

  By closing off your visual connection to the outside world, a whole inner world may show itself to you. Going through the world with our eyes open is like having a flashlight light up the way forward. This practice is like having an inner flashlight lighting the way on our inner journey. It is like walking along a tunnel in a dark cave, our inner eye lighting our way as we wander deeper and deeper into the sacred cave. At times it will be like noticing beautiful and powerful cave art, created thousands of years ago, that is still full of energy and majesty; or like discovering words and poems left by the ancient achieved ones for us to discover on our own journey into the sacred cave.

  Know that your inner journey is just as important, if not more so, than your outer journey through life. Spend at least twenty minutes in this state, not forcing or trying to make anything special happen. Just relax and enjoy the view of your inner world!

- To end this practice, briskly rub your palms (laogong)

together thirty-six times, then place your palms over your eyes and breathe the warmth into your eyes and deep into your brain.

Open your eyes to the world around you but continue to stay in the meditative state for a while. After spending time just being, take a few moments to gather yourself before reentering the world of doing. Enter the rest of your day in a slow and conscious way.

In practicing this way, you will reach what the Daoists call "living midnight," a state of profound mental stillness and quietude that allows our original or celestial mind or spirit to come forth.

23

Full Moon Meditation

THIS IS A SWEET little energy meditation to help you benefit from the full moon, when it is at its peak of yin energy. It can be used when you want to explore the energetic feelings of being calm and centered. It can also help if you are having trouble sleeping or when you just want to find a calm space within yourself. In Chinese mythology the moon is said to be the home of the moon goddess Chang'e. She has a companion called the Jade Rabbit who spends his days pounding a mortar and pestle in order to create the elixir of immortality used by the gods to sustain their immortal lives.

Full Moon Meditation Practice

SIT, STAND, OR LIE DOWN under the full moon. It is especially helpful to be outside, but if that is not possible you can be in front of a window. You just need to be able to see the moon. If this is not possible, you can close your eyes and visualize the full moon floating above your head.

- Begin by naturally breathing in and out of your nose. Allow your breaths to be long, slow, deep, and gentle. You can also experiment with breathing in through your nose, the gate of heaven (*tian men*), and out through your mouth, the door of Earth (*di hu*).

  You can do this meditation when the moon is not full. In that case you will just have to visualize a bright, full moon above your head. Remember, in qigong practice we say "imagination becomes reality," meaning the more you practice, the more real your visualizations will be. In time you will experience all the energetic states in a very real and tactile way.
- As you stand or sit under the moon and gaze upon it, imagine you are filling yourself with its golden glow (sometimes called "moon cream"). Allow the golden, powerful yin energy to fill your body and being. You can also hold your arms out in front of your chest as if you are embracing the moon and say "Ahhhhh."
- Once you have a feeling of fullness between your arms and your chest, move the energy down to your lower dantian, filling it with the good, rich moon cream. Feel it fill your whole body and even your energy or qi field that extends a little way outside of your physical body. Feel the soothing yin energy of the moon filling your whole being with peace and relaxation.
- You also "swallow" the moon cream. Stretch your neck forward a little and fill your mouth with the moon cream while making a swallowing motion, as if you are swallowing a mouthful of water.

- When you are ready to finish, place your palms (laogong) over your lower dantian, palm over palm. Spend a few minutes breathing deeply into your dantian, allowing the yin energy you have gathered from the moon to be sealed into this potent area.

24

Swallowing Saliva Practice

THE SWALLOWING SALIVA PRACTICE (*yan ye*) is very well known in qigong and other Daoist practices in China. But Westerners are often not familiar with it and may find it unappealing in the beginning. It is an important practice and should be done after each qigong or meditation session. To the Daoists, saliva is regarded as a magical elixir, especially when we do the simple practice described in this chapter. Saliva is not a waste product but something our body makes to help with digestion. It is also considered a component of jing (prenatal qi, or the earth body), the first of the Three Treasures (along with qi and shen). In Daoist practice it is referred to as jade dew or divine water. Not only is saliva full of digestive enzymes, hormones, and proteins, but it also has antibacterial properties. By swallowing our saliva, we get the benefit of those enzymes directly into our digestive system.

Yan Ye Practice

THE PRACTICE is very simple. First tap your teeth together thirty-six times. This will help bring more circulation into your gums and strengthen your teeth.

- The first part of the practice is called "the red dragon stirs up the saliva" (*chi long jiao shui jin*). The red dragon is another name for the tongue. With your mouth closed, circle your tongue outside of your teeth thirty-six times to the right, then thirty-six times to the left. This will help create more saliva in your mouth. It will also strengthen your tongue itself. Daoists call this step "turning the red dragon." For a little deeper practice, you can inhale when your tongue is going up across your teeth and exhale when your tongue reaches the bottom of your teeth.
- The next part is called "rouse and rinse the saliva thirty-six times" (*gu xhu san shi liu*). It is also called "evenly fill the mouth with divine water" (*shen shui man kou yun*). Swish the accumulated saliva back and forth in your mouth thirty-six times. This will energize and warm the saliva.
- The final part is called "each mouthful divided into three parts and swallowed" *(yi kou fen san yan)*. Separate the saliva into three parts and swallow each part with a gulping sound. See it in your mind's eye going

all the way down through your esophagus and into your lower dantian. If you are sitting on a meditation cushion or a chair you can place your hands on your thighs with your thumbs inside loose fists.

25

Hall of Light Meditation

THIS MEDITATION WORKS with the upper dantian, or the celestial eye (*tian mu*) and is located between the eyebrows on the forehead. This pressure point is located an inch or so inside our head and is a direct portal to our pineal gland, located deep within our brain. Our pineal gland acts as a tremendous coordinator of our molecular, hormonal, physiological, and chemical rhythmic orchestra.

For many spiritual traditions in the East, our celestial or third eye is said to be linked to perception, awareness, and spiritual communication. This meditation practice is to open our celestial eye and strengthen our psychic abilities.

Hall of Light Meditation Practice

BEGIN YOUR MEDITATION as usual, breathing deeply, slowly, and gently into your lower dantian. Close your eyes to better see with your inner eye.

- Once you feel yourself at peace, allow your focus to come up to your celestial eye. Breathe into this area for a while, feeling your inner eye open like a flower.
- Feel the depth of this point by sending your intention deep into your brain to your pineal gland. As you inhale, breathe golden light into this area. Do this for at least nine deep breaths.
- Then, as you exhale, send out red light into the area in front of you. Send this red light out into the darkness of your spiritual ignorance, lighting the way for you to reach deeper understanding and insight.

  This place you are entering, the inner palace, or the hall of light, is where deep transformation happens. It is where deep healing of the mind and heart happens. It is where you may be gifted with inner vision and psychic perception. You may get some sudden insight into problems or issues that you have been dealing with. You may get some inner knowing that was not available to you before. You may receive some guidance from your higher self, your guiding spirits, or from Dao itself. You may see lights or colors or other visions. Enjoy them but do not hold onto them.
- Take your time with this one. Remember, *manzou,* go slowly. If you are doing this practice at night, be sure to bring your focus back down into your lower dantian to finish. If you leave too much energy in your upper dantian, it may be difficult to fall asleep.

  If you feel dizzy or lightheaded, or if you have a stuffy feeling in your head, you can bring your focus of intention down to the bottom of your feet. If that is not enough, you can also massage the bottom of your feet.

26

Small Heavenly Orbit Meditation

SMALL HEAVENLY ORBIT (*xiao zhou tian*) is an ancient practice designed to start transforming the earthly energy of jing to the purer energy of qi and is also called "returning the essence to replenish the brain." It opens two of our major qi channels to allow qi to flow more clearly and strongly, empowering us to call on greater reserves of energy as we need it, and leading to a state of inner peace, greater health, and transformation. It is a bit more advanced than many of the other practices in this book so you will need to go slowly. Be gentle with yourself. Remember the principle of wu wei: not forcing, not overdoing!

The two major qi channels, or meridians, in our body, the du mai, or back channel, and the *ren mai*, or front channel, can be thought of as the major highways of the qi system. These, along with the chong mai, or central channel that runs from the top of our head (the baihui pressure point) down through the center of our body to our perineum (*hui yin*), contain the biggest flow of qi in our body. Like major highways in the world, they can get overcrowded; qi may back up, just like car traffic. When this happens our qi moves in a tight and sluggish way and may result in lots of health problems, from slight to serious. We need to get our qi moving again by guiding qi with our mind and breath so that it moves freely and speedily again. Remember the principle "qi follows yi" or "qi flows where the mind goes." This practice uses mindful intention to affect real change in our body—physical as well as spiritual.

Put another way, the du mai that runs up our back is yang; the ren mai that runs down our front is yin. A blockage or stagnation in either of these two channels will cause an imbalance in our yin/yang energy, which can lead to all kinds of health problems. When doing this practice it is important to place the tip of your tongue to the roof of your mouth, as we have been doing in our other practices. This will link up the du mai and ren mai, completing the circuit.

There are twelve major points up the back and down the front of our body that qi needs to move through. Gently guide your qi up through each point on your back, then down the front of your body, stopping to breathe at least nine times into each point. As you go through each one, see the point or the area in your mind's eye softening, opening, and lighting up. Once you get through all twelve of them, your qi body will be like a lit-up Christmas tree! It should take around thirty minutes to go through the whole circuit three times. If you have less time or want a slower way into the practice, you can go through the entire circuit two times or even once, but the more time you spend on it the more powerful the practice will be. When you are done you should guide your qi very gently up the du mai and then down the ren mai, back into your lower dantian. Do this at least nine times.

In this next practice we will be doing reverse breathing. Instead of allowing our lower abdomen to expand with each inhalation, we will do the opposite and contract our abdomen with each inhale and relax it with each exhale. This kind of breathing is done when we want to build or strengthen our qi system. Remember to breathe into each point at least nine times. In the beginning you will be using your imagination to move the qi, but eventually, if you are constant with your practice, you will feel the qi moving on its own.

Small Heavenly Orbit or Lesser Celestial Circuit Practice

WE BEGIN by sitting in stillness, our breath coming and going like a door opening and closing.

- Put your mindful intention (*yi*) into your lower dantian. Breathe slowly and deeply and feel your field of elixir become full of qi.
- Focus on your lower dantian. Spend some time breathing and filling your dantian with good, rich qi.
- Guide your intention to your perineum. Feel this place soften and begin lighting up. Breathe into this area nine times.

- Guide your qi up to the bottom of your tailbone or coccyx (*wei lu*). Breathe into this area nine times.
- Guide your qi up to your lower back, between your kidneys (the gate of destiny, *ming men*). Breathe into this area nine times.
- Guide your qi up to your middle back, opposite your heart center (*ling tai*). Breathe into this area nine times.
- Guide your qi up to the big bone at the top of your spine (da zhui). Breathe into this area nine times.
- Guide your qi up to the base of your skull, the *yu zhen*, also called the jade pillow. Breathe into this area nine times.
- Guide your qi up to the very top of your head to the baihui pressure point. Breathe into this area nine times. This is a very potent point. Often, when your baihui begins to open, it will feel like tiny ants walking across the top of your head. If this happens it is important not to scratch, as it will cause the point to close again.
- Guide your qi down to your celestial eye (upper dantian). Breathe into this area nine times.
- Guide your qi down to the magpie bridge, under your nose. Breathe into this area nine times.
- Guide your qi down to the bottom of your throat (*xuan jing*). Breathe into this area nine times.
- Guide your qi down to the middle dantian (the crimson palace). Breathe into this area nine times.
- To finish, put your intention back into your belly, your

lower dantian, and relax into a state of mindfulness and gratitude.

After doing this practice for some time, you may feel a tingling or a sense of warmth as the qi rises, descends, and begins to work its way through whatever blockages you may have in these areas. Just remember to go slowly, gently guiding the qi with your mind and not forcing anything to happen.

27

Crimson Palace Meditation

IN THIS MEDITATION we will balance, clear, harmonize, and strengthen the middle dantian, located at the center of our chest between our nipples. We are cultivating a light or radiant spirit (*xin ming*). As we saw in the organ balancing meditation, the heart is associated with the color red, hence the name crimson palace. In traditional Chinese medicine, the heart is considered the emperor of all the other organs. It is also the seat of our shen, or spiritual self, and is sometimes called "the abode of the spirit." The heart is often depicted as a lotus flower with three petals.

The Daoists say that that our cognitive mind also dwells in the heart. When someone is in a very deep state of psychosis, they are thought of as having a disturbed shen. Short-term memory loss, insomnia, and too much vivid dreaming are all thought of as unbalanced or disturbed shen conditions.

Our heart is not just a blood pump; it sends electrical signals and messages to the brain in what is called "heart-brain synchronization." The heart is actually an information processing center that sends important messages throughout our entire body. It starts beating in the unborn fetus before the brain has formed. It is indeed the seat of emotional intelligence that is important to nourish. This meditation practice is one simple way to do that.

The *Neijing,* an ancient book on Chinese medicine, says "When the heart is at peace, all the organs are at peace." Yet so often our heart and our mind are not at peace but are filled with desires, apprehensions, worries, and fears. The wild horse of our mind is running wildly about, moving madly around in circles but getting nowhere. This meditation and many of the others in this book address this issue.

It is important to spend at least fifteen to twenty minutes with this meditation. You may find that you need to spend even longer if you are having a problem or a deficiency in a particular organ or area. Keep in mind that we are not trying to *force* anything to happen but to gently *allow* the practices to affect your whole body and being—energetically, physically, emotionally, psychologically, and even spiritually.

Crimson Palace Meditation Practice

START BY DOING a few minutes of lower-dantian breathing. Let your focus ascend to dwell on the middle dantian.

- As you inhale feel your heart open and expand outward; and as you exhale feel it open and expand inward.
- Continue to breathe in and out in this way, feeling

your heart center expanding into each direction.

- In your mind's eye, see a ball or field of crimson light in front of you.
- On your next inhalation allow this crimson light to fill your heart, purging it of all concerns and worries.
- Let your spirit feel light and easy. Feel your whole being fill with light and clear energy. This energetic state, when our hearts are full of light, will travel to all parts of our body and being, helping us to maintain a positive attitude throughout our lives.
- Continue in this way for a while, feeling your heart center expanding inwardly and outwardly, giving you a feeling of safety, lightness, and joy. Remember that the heart organ is associated with joy, expansion, and creativity. Allow yourself to align with these potent emotional and energetic states.

28

Tranquil Sitting

ZHUANGZI SAYS that we live in a dream state even though we may think we are awake. It might be a good dream or a bad dream. When we dream we think the dream is real; when we wake up we realize it was just a dream, and now we are awake in the so-called real world. To the Daoists, almost everything we see and experience in our so-called waking life is part of the dream that we call "living." All of our problems and challenges are part of this dreaming. Not only that, but our attempts to break out of the dream are also part of the dream.

There is a famous story about Zhuangzi. He dreamed he was a butterfly and then awakened, not sure if he was a man who had dreamed he was a butterfly or a butterfly who now dreamed he was a man! Waking up from this dreaming is the path of letting go of all self-limiting ideas, fears, and habits.

We do this tranquil sitting meditation with a light heart and open mind. We sit with a feeling of joy and a spirit of letting go of anything we don't need in order to reach a state of deep inner peace. Laozi says,

> *Tranquil stillness balances*
> *all things under heaven.*[21]

The goal of this practice, as with many of the other practices in this book, is to create a space or field of tranquility and peace so that we can bring that feeling into the rest of our lives. As I mentioned earlier, the more we do these practices, the stronger our meditation muscles will be and the easier it will be to drop down into states of peace and tranquility.

Tranquil Sitting Meditation

SIT ON YOUR CUSHION OR CHAIR, align your limbs, and allow a feeling of joy and a lightness of spirit. Relax your face muscles into a small smile. As you sit in meditation, don't try to stop the mad monkey or wild horse of your thoughts, but don't give in to them either. Sit with the goal of waking up, of letting go of the bonds that hold you down and restrict your movement between the physical and spiritual worlds. This is a time to let go of bad habits, fears, laziness, or anything that is holding you back from waking up.

Sit with fierce determination as well as soft, joyful acceptance of yourself exactly as you are right now. Sit up straight; do not slump, yet do not hold yourself too rigidly either. Just sit like a happy child, with a relaxed mind and heart. The more straight your spine is the easier it will be for qi to travel throughout your body and being. Remember to breathe slowly, deeply, and gently. Allow your mind and spirit to dance on the waves of your breath.

Follow the watercourse way and flow with the dream, all the while knowing that the dream is not real. In this way you will be one of those whom the ancient Daoists called “seed people” (*zhongmin*). Seed people are the ones who advise others on how to wake up. They have already woken up, sometimes in another lifetime. They have come here in this lifetime to remind us of who we really are. You may be one of these seed people right now!

When you enter the realm of tranquil sitting, allow the seed person you truly are to emerge!

———

29

Internal Alchemy Meditation

IN ANCIENT CHINA, just as in Europe, people practiced alchemy in order to transform base metals into gold. Unlike Europeans, who were trying to create gold as a form of money, the Chinese were trying to create gold to make bowls and plates. It was believed that if someone ate off gold plates, the gold would allow them to live a long life free of disease.

There was also a great interest in creating a pill of immortality. This was of great interest to the emperor, who wanted to keep his job forever. The problem was that a lot of these pills contained highly toxic ingredients, such as lead and mercury, that killed a number of emperors!

After a lengthy period of experimenting in this way (*waidan*, or external alchemy), the ancient Daoist alchemists decided to stop these practices and instead focus on the energies that are inherent in our bodies and qi systems—neidan, or inner alchemy. After much inner exploration and experimenting, they created the nurturing life practices (*yang sheng*) that include things like qigong, meditation, herbology, taiji, and other traditional Chinese medicine practices.

In neidan practice we refine the energy of our qi, or life-force energy, using breath, movement, visualization, meditation, and movement practices to become not an immortal but a very strong and healthy person. The following meditation is a short introduction to this fascinating tradition of energy healing.

Internal Alchemy Meditation

SIT OR STAND, relaxing your whole body and being from the top of your head to the bottom of your feet.

- Place your focus on your lower dantian. Place the tip of your tongue to the roof of your mouth. Close your eyes so that you can see with your inner eye. Begin breathing slowly, deeply, and gently through your nose. Imagine that you are actually breathing in and out of your lower dantian. Spend a few moments just breathing in this way, feeling very relaxed and centered.
- Then, in your mind's eye, see a golden ball of qi rotating clockwise in your lower dantian. See it and feel it revolving in your lower dantian, full of condensed healing energy.
- As you inhale and your abdomen expands, feel the ball getting larger and stronger. As you exhale and your abdomen contracts, feel the golden qi ball condensing to a smaller but even more potent ball.

  You can play with the golden ball a little, experimenting with two ways of working with it. Instead of expanding on your inhale, allow it to contract and condense with each inhale and expand on your exhale. You may experience more qi moving with one or the other. When you find the one that works best for you, stick with it for a little while.

- Continue to inhale and exhale, allowing the golden ball to expand and then condense. Feel it growing stronger and more powerful as it spreads its healing qi throughout your body. Keep breathing and allowing (though not forcing) this ball of golden qi to expand and condense until you feel its healing qi spreading and filling your whole body and being.

  You can also direct its healing light to anywhere in your body you have pain, disease, or stress—mentally, physically, emotionally, or even psychically. This is alchemy at a very high level. Alchemy is the practice of transformation, of changing something small to something large, of bringing light to the darkness, of allowing inner healing to take place.
- You may experience some movement at this time. It can be a gentle shaking or larger movements. Don't try to control them, but don't try to stop them unless they become uncomfortable. If you become uncomfortable, you can easily stop the movements by just telling yourself to stop. This type of undirected movement is called "spontaneous qigong." You may experience emotional release at this time as well. Don't get upset if you begin crying or even laughing. This is all well and good.

Your movements may be small, or they may be big. You may move very slowly, or you may even jerk around. As long as it is not your mind that is telling you how to move, it is fine. Let your own qi tell you how to move. Your mind may not understand what the qi of your body is doing at this time. Just relax and enjoy it.

- To end the meditation, do the saliva swallowing practice (chapter 24). Then rub your palms together thirty-six times and place them over your eyes. Breathe the warmth of your palms (laogong) into your eyes and all the way into your brain.

  Then take a few moments to just sit in noble silence, allowing all the inner alchemical work to come to rest within your lower abdomen and throughout your whole body and being.

AFTERWORD

THESE PRACTICES may seem simple, but they are very powerful and can affect your whole body and being. You can experiment with a few of them to find the ones that speak to you the most and focus on them. Then, at another time, you might discover that some other practices are more appropriate for you.

Some of these practices are very old, even ancient. Laozi wrote the *Daodejing* 2,500 years ago, and even then he often mentioned the ancient masters. They are the 5,000-year-old lineage of teachers of Dao, many of them from various shamanic (*wu*) traditions.

It might seem strange to practice breathing into your lower abdomen, swallowing saliva as a magical elixir, or to accept the idea that both positive and negative emotional states are associated with your various organs. But these practices and ideas have really stood the test of time and can work for us just as well as for the ancient Daoists.

Remember, you do not have to convert to Daoism to utilize any of these practices. Most important, take your time and have fun with them!

NOTES

1. Solala Towler, *Practicing the Tao Te Ching: 81 Steps on the Way* (Sounds True, 2016), 64.
2. Hua-Ching Ni, *Spring Thunder: Awaken the Hibernating Power of Life* (SevenStar Communications, 1996), 104.
3. Hua-Ching Ni, *The Gentle Path of Spiritual Progress* (SevenStar Communications, 2009), 85.
4. Chuang Tzu, *The Inner Chapters: The Classic Taoist Text,* trans. Solala Towler (Watkins, 2011), 99.
5. Towler, *Practicing the Tao Te Ching,* 45.
6. Towler, *Practicing the Tao Te Ching,* 67.
7. Hua-Ching Ni, *The Centermost Way* (SevenStar Communications, 2001), 29.
8. Huangdi was a legendary ruler who ascended to power in 2697 B.C.E. and is seen as a great cultural hero of China.
9. John Blofeld, *The Secret and Sublime: Taoist Mysteries and Magic* (Shambhala Publications, 1973), 13–14.
10. Towler, *Practicing the Tao Te Ching,* 87.
11. Towler, *Practicing the Tao Te Ching,* 67.
12. Stuart Alve Olson, *Clarity & Tranquility: A Guide for Daoist Meditation,* ed. Patrick D. Gross (Valley Spirit Arts, 2015), 58.
13. Tzu, *The Inner Chapters,* 74.
14. Hua-Ching Ni, *Workbook for Spiritual Development* (Tao of Wellness, 1992), 124.

15. For more on the directions, colors, emotional states, and power animals, see chapter 12, "Organ Balancing Meditation."
16. Towler, *Practicing the Tao Te Ching*, 24.
17. Tzu, *The Inner Chapters*, 76.
18. Wu De, *Tea Medicine* (Global Tea Hut, 2014), 5.
19. Paul Rosenberg, personal interview with author.
20. Zhongxian Wu, *Vital Breath of the Dao* (Singing Dragon, 2021), 9.
21. Towler, *Practicing the Tao Te Ching*, 162.

ABOUT THE AUTHOR

Solala Towler is the author of fourteen books, including:

A Gathering of Cranes: Bringing the Tao to the West (Abode of the Eternal Dao)
Cha Dao: The Way of Tea, Tea as a Way of Life (Singing Dragon)
The Inner Chapters: The Classic Taoist Text (Watkins)
Tales from the Tao: The Wisdom of the Tao Masters (Watkins)
The Tao of Intimacy and Ecstasy: Realizing the Promise of Spiritual Union (Sounds True)
Tea Heart Tea Mind: A Journey Through the Dao of Tea (Abode of the Eternal Dao)
Practicing the Tao Te Ching: 81 Steps on the Way (Sounds True)
The Spirit of Zen: The Classic Teaching Stories on the Way to Enlightenment (Watkins)

Solala teaches qigong, Daoist meditation, and tea ceremony at workshops and conferences in the United States; and he leads tours to China and Taiwan to explore qigong, tea ceremony, and Daoist meditation in the sacred mountains.

For more information on Solala's China trips, his books, and his workshops and classes, write to solala@abodetao.com or go to his website at www.abodetao.com.